YOUR SECOND FIFTY

Live Your Life to the Fullest

YOUR SECOND FIFTY

Live Your Life to the Fullest

FRANK MOFFATT

PT Elex Media Komputindo
KOMPAS GRAMEDIA

YOUR SECOND FIFTY

Live Your Life to the Fullest

Written by Frank Moffatt

First Published by PT Elex Media Komputindo Publishing Company
Kompas Gramedia Group
IKAPI member, Jakarta

236091849
ISBN:978-979-27-5914-3

Mind, Body & Soul

Foreword

This book is more a collaboration of hundreds of people, their writings, their wisdom and their courage to question previous beliefs and to look positively and progressively into the future. I hope that these efforts, will hopefully lead you to explore your own unlimited potentialities and to come to the realization that given the time and effort a fantastic, fulfilling second fifty years is well within your control. To all of you that have inspired me and shown me the path to my unlimited potential I say thanks.

People can only learn when their original assumptions have been broken.

Steve Chang – Founder, Trend Micro

To Michael Pond, thank you for your inspiration, ideas and guidance pertaining to the layout of this book, for your feedback on various chapters, for providing me with a quality writing environment and for offering me employment which allowed me to continue to write and cover my basic needs and expenses. Without your help this book would not have become a reality.

To Dale Wallace, you are the man! Editing my run-on sentences so that the readers wouldn't be hyperventilating by the second chapter is an amazing feat in of itself. But to assist me to orchestrate all of these little snippets of information into that of a book, now that's something - wow!

To my sons, thank you for your unconditional love

and support. You are truly amazing young men; you have taught me so much. I wish you well as you continue to blaze your own paths throughout your journeys. To my family and friends, thank you for your spiritual guidance, wisdom and diversity in acceptance, compassion and understanding.

In the words of Alan Cohen:

It takes a lot of courage to release the familiar and seemingly secure, to embrace the new. But there is no real security in what is no longer meaningful. There is more security in the adventurous and exciting, for in movement there is life, and in change there is power.

Special Thanks!

To Indra, Paulina, Lucia and all the kind people at PT Elex Media Komputindo, Kompas Gramedia Group that helped put this text to paper. To Yunia, Ronny, Bob, Sandip, Bill and Mike for your never ending support. To Raksit Rakkandee for the artistic touch on the 50 Fantastic Days. To Prapaichit Potpan for performing magic with your camera. To Patcharee Poosommai for your creative layout ideas.

Check Us Out!

Your Second Fifty Online - www.yoursecondfifty.net; Your Second Fifty Magazine (English) - www.yoursecondfifty.com; Your Second Fifty Magazine (Indonesian) - www.yoursecondfifty.com/indonesia; Your Second Fifty Online Community - www.ysffamilybook.com

Email: yoursecondfifty@yahoo.com; yoursecondfifty@gmail.com; yoursecondfifty@hotmail.com

Table of Contents

Introduction

At age 95, Nola Ochs became the world's oldest college graduate. At age 94 Fauja Singh competed in the Edinburgh Marathon Relay. Jeanne Calment of France died at 122 years of age. Nerve cells in the human brain and muscle cells in the heart have the capacity to last more than 100 years. So why do our bodies break down and the majority of us die before we reach 100 years of age? Because most of us believe that's just the way it is suppose to be.

I could not, at any age, be content to take my place by the fireside and simply look on. Life was meant to be lived. Curiosity must be kept alive. One must never, for whatever reason, turn his back on life.

Eleanor Roosevelt

In this book we intend to challenge **traditional** beliefs and present to you an alternative way of thinking. The information provided within this book is only a guide; the journey is yours. Our belief is that when our mental, emotional, physical and spiritual dimensions are in balance a long and healthy second fifty years is unquestionably within our reach.

We will open the endless possibilities that lay before you. Yet, we do not intend to lecture or preach. Rather, we will simply and humbly offer a path through the four dimensions of your life: the mental, emotional, physical, and spiritual. It is essential to understand that before you begin this journey that you are prepared to challenge old beliefs and explore new possibilities. If you are willing to have an open mind, you will discover that the capacity to completely change your own experience of ageing lies within you.

Life is an endless series of challenges and hurdles and the key to successfully addressing and confronting those challenges is discipline. However, the manner in which you address your challenges will determine the degree of your successes or failures. Those who have experienced true success have accepted that pain is a natural part of living and a key component in overcoming life`s challenges. This newly attained wisdom will serve you well as you continue to apply self-discipline to life's ongoing journey. Be aware that your life is in your hands and you are ultimately responsible.

Society has become geared for the quick fix, heaping great praise on the experts that proclaim, "Here's the problem - here's the magic pill!" Nothing could be further from the truth when attempting life changes. These experts don't change us - we change ourselves. We change ourselves by accepting, surrendering, and then taking corrective action.

Half our life is spent trying to find something to do with the time, we have rushed through life trying to save.

Will Rogers

Our mental, emotional, physical and spiritual lives are intricately linked, and when one or more of these areas are ignored the holistic result (our self) is out of balance and lacks cohesion. To use an analogy, if one tire on a car is low of air pressure and out of balance, the subsequent poor performance of that tire directly influences the overall performance of the entire vehicle. Or, for example if a woman were to train five hours a week in the gym with aspirations of shapely hips and legs, but perceived herself with a pear shaped figure, she would be pretty much guaranteed little chance of attaining her physical goals. Thus we need to positively align our mental capacities, emotional states, and spiritual practices with our physical goals, for our full potential to be realized.

Question Your Thinking

A young woman was preparing a ham dinner. After she cut off the end of the ham, she placed it in a pan for baking. Her friend asked her, "Why did you cut off the end of the ham"? And she replied, "I really don't know but my mother always did, so I thought you were supposed to."

Later when talking to her mother she asked her why she cut off the end of the ham before baking it and her mother replied, "I really don't know, but that's the way my mom always did it."

A few weeks later while visiting her grandmother, the young woman asked, "Grandma, why is it that you cut off the end of a ham before you bake it?"

Her grandmother replied, "Well dear, it would never fit into my baking pan."

We have always been taught that ageing is irreversible and that a progressive decline in our mental, emotional, and physical capacities is a natural process. In Your Second 50 we invite you to consider the option of changing the way you think about aging and experience for yourself the reality of a revitalized and rejuvenated self.

Deepak Chopra says that our minds have been conditioned to believe that the normal experience of the body and its ageing is a habit of our thinking and behaviour and that by changing how we think and behave, we can change our mind's and our body's experience of ageing.

Harvard psychologist, Ellen Langer, took groups of men in their seventies and eighties who were encouraged to behave and think as if they were twenty years younger. These men showed definite physical changes of much younger men after only five days. Thus, if we have the mental and emotional expectation that we are younger and will live longer we will live up to that expectation.

In the book BioMarkers by William Evans, researchers have medically proven that the body is constantly rebuilding itself and can actually grow younger with the right conditions. So the reality is that if you change your way of thinking, your emotional states, your physical fitness, and your spiritual practices then your body and mind will experience regeneration, renewal, and revitalization.

Quantum physics theory* compels us to change how we view the whole process of life, the human body, and ageing. At the quantum level, the potential for regrowth and renewal is beyond the scope of our human imagination and understanding. However, it suggests that our essence, or who we really are, is beyond the mental and physical realms. That is, from the perspective of quantum physics, the spiritual realm of existence is the cornerstone for improving our mental, physical, and emotional health. The spiritual domain is the true source of all our happiness, freedom, joy, and sense of fulfillment. Quantum physicists herald that we all have the capacity to alter our physical body and the functioning of our minds. Some scientists now

* Quantum physics is a branch of science that deals with discrete, indivisible units of energy called quanta as described by the Quantum Theory. Quantum theory is the theoretical basis of modern physics that explains the nature and behaviour of matter and energy on the atomic and subatomic level.

believe that we can determine and change the biological age and physiological condition that we want our body and mind to be in.

Now some of these ideas may be difficult for you to accept. However, for you to grow mentally, emotionally, physically, and spiritually you must be willing to consider new research that disproves previously accepted beliefs based upon folklore, myths, and outdated research. These concepts are new and challenging but within our reach if we can discard the naysayer's comments and believe in our potentialities. The Wright Brothers believed in possibilities and flight became a reality. It all comes down to personal faith in our ability to succeed in what we believe in. However, to better understand and accept this new way of thinking, it's important to understand the three types of age classifications and how age is categorized. These classifications include the following: chronological age, biological age and psychological age.

Chronological age is the number of years that have passed in our lives starting from the date of our birth and the subsequent passage of time according to the annual calendar. This age cannot be changed. Ironically, chronological age is the least significant factor in determining how old we feel or function.

Biological age is the measure of how well our physiological systems are functioning. Our biological age is calculated through biological markers; some of which include body fat composition, cholesterol levels, blood pressure, aerobic functioning, and bone density. As expected, our biological age can be the same as or differ significantly from our chronological age. In other words, an individual who is chronologically fifty years of age can be functioning biologically at a much younger age or a much older age dependant on the way they live their life. People who take care of themselves can have a younger biological age; whereas, an individual who is sedentary and has poor eating habits can have an older chronological age.

Psychological age is our own personal experience of how old we feel. So if we tap into the energy that determines how old we feel our body can actually become younger by utilizing different mental capacities. Thus, how we think we feel can actually determine how young or old we are. The most significant factor in determining how old we actually feel and function is our attitude. This attitude translates into the saying "growing older means growing better." If we believe and expect our mental and physical capacities to diminish with age, they probably will. On the other hand, if we believe and expect that we can attain youthful vitality, our experience will most likely follow that course of thought.

Michael Pond R.P.N., M.S.W.

Hopefully by now your interest has been piqued and you have come to the conclusion, "What do I have to lose, by giving this a try?" The answer, "Nothing but a little fear based comfort!" However, that little fear actually has the capacity to completely immobilize us. So how do we overcome that fear? The answer is by self-discipline. By self-disciple we are referring to our ability to apply our willpower over the execution and completion of a given task, even though we would rather be doing something else.

Then we need to set attainable goals that we are comfortable with, and goals that will provide us with long term, lasting results. Once we have a solid understanding of discipline and goals we can begin the process of exploring the countless opportunities of enhancing our four dimensions.

The first dimension we will explore and learn to enhance is the Mental Dimension. The Mental Dimension encompasses all aspects of consciousness and intellect and is manifested through any combination of thought, imagination, perception, memory, or will. In other words our Mental Dimension provides us with the capability to reason – the unaided ability to form concepts, to analyze, or to study. By shifting the Mental Dimension alone we can completely change our lives.

Live your life, forget your age.
Norman Vincent Peale

The second dimension we will address is the Emotional Dimension. The Emotional Dimension encompasses ones ability, skill, or capacity to assess, perceive, and manage one's emotions. It is our own experience of our feelings and what we do with those feelings that is the manifestation of how we perceive ourselves and how others perceive us.

The third dimension covered will be the Physical Dimension. The Physical Dimension pertains to our material being and bodily functions. These components encompass not only our aerobic fitness, our muscle strength/endurance, and our flexibility, but also our nutrition, diet, and how we effectively care for our bodies.

The fourth dimension is our Spiritual Dimension. The Spiritual Dimension relates to our faith and beliefs, our willingness to accept a higher power, our commitment to an honourable value system, and the laws of nature. This dimension, for some of us, can be the most difficult to accept and understand, yet it is the most significant and powerful dimension of the four.

In *Your Second 50* we will give you a fifty day program of activities and inspirational readings that will form a solid four dimensional foundation for a second fifty years of youthful health and vigour. Life is what we make of it. We all have had hard days, and everyone is faced with challenges and extreme difficulties throughout life. However, if we provide equal attention to all four dimensions in our life, each will act as a support system for the other and provide us with the complete internal strength necessary to continue. Patiently and persistently, one step at a time, as each dimension grows stronger, all dimensions grow stronger, and the individual grows stronger too.

Twenty years from now you will be more disappointed by the things you didn't do than by the ones you did do. So throw off the bowlines. Sail away from the safe harbor. Catch the trade winds in your sails.

Explore. Dream Discover.

Mark Twain

If you persevere you will be bound to succeed. Thomas Edison said that perseverance is the secret to success. It took him thousands of trials to successfully invent the incandescent light bulb. It took the inventor de Mestral eight years of trial and error until he developed a successful design for Velcro. As with all good things, success begins one step at a time, and before we know it something magical has happened.

It is our sincere hope that this book opens new doors and inspires you to challenge yourself and your unlimited capacity to live a healthy, balanced, and fulfilling second fifty years. So now let's get started, because today is the first day of the rest of your life and whatever happened in our past plays no role what-so-ever now or in the future.

The Frank Experience – Introduction

Fifty-three years of age, or at least that's how old I was at the time of writing this book, hardly makes me an expert at living to 100. However, after all the research that I've done and all those with whom I've spoken too that are happy and healthy well into their second fifty, I'm convinced that given discipline and effort the rewards of a healthy, happy and balanced second fifty years are well within our reach.

Each of us starts on the same playing field and the only difference is our perceived view of ourselves and others.

We don't have a disadvantage unless we are informed we have a disadvantage, and then we must accept and believe in this disadvantage in order to actualize this disadvantage. Great men and women weren't awarded their talents they are a product of their diligence, effort and it persistence. It isn't luck and it isn't chance. Success comes from hard work and persistence.

You've got to live it – to live!

Frank Moffatt

Leonardo da Vinci, Albert Einstein and Bill Gates represent exceptional mental dimensions. Martin Luther King Jr., Mother Theresa and Nelson Mandela demonstrate extraordinary emotional dimensions. Jesse Owens, Terry Fox and Wayne Gretzky illustrate astonishing physical dimensions and The Buddha, Jesus of Nazareth and Muhammad exemplify undeniable spiritual dimensions. None of them attained their place in history because it was their God given right—they went out and lived their passion one day at a time and as with everything else in life—staying focused, putting in the time and living life to the best of their ability paid off in them actualizing their dreams.

So, is it important for each of us to become worldly renown as a great mind, a pillar in the face of adversity, a champion of champions, or a worshiped spiritual figure? I think not, but I do believe it's important to challenge ourselves daily and to do everything in our power to be the best we can be. At the same time it is important to discipline ourselves to overcome our innately lazy tendencies to waste our only truly precious commodity – our time, and in turn, our lives.

Discipline

> *In reading the lives of great men, I found that the first victory they won was over themselves...*
> *self-discipline with all of them came first."*
>
> Harry S Truman

While it certainly does appear that our future looks exceeding bright, the road to attaining these rewards will be difficult and at times down right uncomfortable. So how will we overcome these difficulties? Discipline! Or more precisely - self-discipline. Self-discipline is the act of disciplining ourselves to do what it takes to have what we want even though we would prefer to be doing something else or nothing at all.

Life is difficult. This is a great truth; one of the greatest truths. It is a great truth because once we truly see this truth, we transcend it. Once we truly know that life is difficult – once we truly understand and accept it – then life is no longer difficult.

Because once it is accepted, the fact that life is difficult no longer matters. *

Scott Peck

However, for most of us Peck's idea is almost impossible to accept because if we accept his idea, we are then compelled to accept that we are completely responsible for our own experience of life. Most people have difficulty accepting responsibility for the results

* The first of the "Four Noble Truths" which Buddha taught was "Life is suffering."

If you do not conquer self, you will be conquered by self.

Napoleon Hill

of their choices and the decisions that they make. Instead, they prefer to believe that it is the actions of others that cause their pain and suffering. However, once they neglect or relegate to others (blame) the consequences of their choices, they no longer have to take responsibility. Without taking responsibility we can't effectively apply a solution.

So how do we accept and apply self-discipline in our lives? First, we must be willing to delay gratification. We need to eat our dinner before we eat our dessert; we need to complete the task at hand no matter how challenging before we take a break; we need to overcome our natural instinct to run from mental or physical pain. Delaying gratification is becoming more and more of a challenge today because of instantaneous marketing and the perception that there is a quick simple fix for everything. Computers can fix our grammar, talk show hosts have countless guests with quick fixes for all our emotions, plastic surgeons suck away our fat, and televangelist dissolve our misdeeds for the week with one quick outburst of words on Sunday morning. In fact we are now conditioned to look for the quick fix because we need that immediate payoff. But the truth is everything that is important takes time and while a quick fix gives us instantaneous gratification, without continued work, diligence, and commitment our misery is certain to find its way back. Sadly, the pain we were looking to eradicate has actually only been suppressed.

Second, we must be willing to accept responsibility. We must accept that we are completely in control of how we respond and react to all the events in our lives. No one limits our ability to learn but ourselves. We may not learn as quickly as others, but if we put the time in we will most certainly learn whatever it is we are attempting to learn.

hird, we must be dedicated to the truth. This statement isn't easy because we have all been taught to justify, manipulate, and twist the truth to suit our needs. But truth is reality and anything unreal is then false. So anything that has not yet transpired can only be unreal and a figment of our imagination as concocted by our ego. If we are over weight the truth is we ate more food than our body required. It's that simple. (Thyroid Foundation of Canada states - The safest approach is lifestyle modification that results in decreased caloric intake by changing eating habits and increased expenditure of calories by exercising more. Even though weight control may be more difficult after being diagnosed with hypothyroidism, it is still quite possible.)

With self-discipline most anything is possible.

Theodore Roosevelt

Self-respect is the fruit of discipline: the sense of dignity grows with the ability to say no to oneself.

Abraham Heschel

Finally, we must live a life of balance. Balance means we are willing to adjust to each situation, to remain flexible, and to consider that not everything is possible all of the time. Highs make lows and lows make highs. If we want equanimity in our lives we need to keep ourselves balanced.

Procrastination is the fear of success. People procrastinate because they are afraid of the success that they know will result if they move ahead now. Because success is heavy, carries a responsibility with it, it is much easier to procrastinate and live on the 'someday I'll' philosophy.

Denis Waitley

Initially, self-discipline may appear as a hardship full of pain and frustration, but the reality couldn't be anything further from the truth. Mastery of self-discipline not only leads us out of internal frustration and pain but into genuine self confidence and satisfaction. We are capable of achieving whatever we want whenever we want once we put our minds to it.

The Frank Experience - Discipline

For me discipline has always been a difficult hurdle because I'm always looking for the easiest, shortest, and quickest way out of every situation. Sadly, I'm usually trying with words and not actions. However, interestingly enough, everything that I've ever accomplished in my life is directly related to me asserting my will on a consistent basis and remaining focused on my primary goal, which in turn equals the act of self discipline.

For example, when I was in my 52nd year I decided I was going to run a marathon. For a guy that grew up with asthma and could barely make the four laps prior to a football practice, I don't know what ever came over me and lead me to this idea. But once it was in place, the act of discipline not only became a requirement it became a necessity.

Every morning I got up at 6:00 am put on my shorts, shirt, and runners and took off out the door. I began training by running one kilometer a day, although for the first few days half of the kilometer was spent walking. I despised the first couple of hundred meters, but I told myself that it would get better. Because I didn't give in, because I never quite, and because I was disciplined, over time the training got easier.

By the end of the first month I was up to three kilometers a day. My blisters had become calluses and my gut had quit jiggling – or should I say bouncing. During the second month I had moved up to five kilometers twice a week, and trust me I was still counting every single step.

The third month I had pushed one of my weekly five k runs up to eight kilometers, but was now taking two days off a week to recuperate. That's what I read in a training article, and who am I to argue with the professionals. The fourth month I was putting in a ten k run every second Saturday, and some days everything just clicked. I actually felt like a runner.

During the fifth month I did one twenty kilometer run three weeks in advance of the race. After that run I really questioned myself. Was I completely nuts? Twenty kilometers wasn't even half way I needed to run the marathon, plus I was nearly crawling by the end of the twenty kilometers. But on November 27, 2005 (down twelve Kilo's from when I started), I crossed the finish line in 4.29.51 and in the top 100 for my age classification of 50 – 54 years of age. So will I ever do that again? I doubt it, but over my first fifty years I've learned the dangers in saying the word "never." I still run on occasion, but now I prefer to walk between four and six kilometers a day.

Currently, I am disciplining myself to pursue the art of yoga. I can clearly see the benefits; I just need to maintain self discipline, perseverance, and patience to overcome my rigidity. That being said, we all need to set aside our preconceived notions that stop us from taking action that will help us to physically enjoy the second fifty years of our lives.

Setting Goals

> *Setting goals is the first step in turning the invisible into the visible.*
>
> Anthony Robbins

Would we take a two-week vacation without having any idea where we were going? Even if we had no specific destination, most of us would at least consult a map or tourist guide of the region in which we were traveling. So then why do most of us live our personal lives without any form of organized direction? As stated earlier, it boils down to avoiding the fear and pain associated with all the effort, discipline, and time required to reach our unrealistic dreams. The reason we say "unrealistic" is because too often our dreams are based upon past or current results of another person and our visual images of what they have attained. That doesn't mean these dreams aren't possible. It just means that for each of us our starting points in all four dimensions are unique to us, and we need to be extremely careful not to overload ourselves before we have any idea of what we are getting into. That being said, we still need dreams, as dreams or visions are the first step of any endeavour or plan we intend to embark upon. However, like our vacation, our dreams need a roadmap and that road map is called setting goals.

Setting goals is the key for motivating ourselves and turning our dreams or visions into reality. The pro-

If you don't know where you are going, you'll end up some-place else.

Yogi Berra

cess of setting goals helps us clearly see the direction in which we need to go, how far we need to go in an allotted period of time and to keep us focused and on course. At the same time, we are clearly defining the hazards or distractions that normally lead us down the wrong road. As well, setting and achieving goals can be incredibly motivating and an effective self-confidence builder.

In absence of clearly defined goals, we become strangely loyal to performing daily acts of trivia.

Author Unknown

Goal setting is the ultimate high. Successful business people, world class athletes, and, in fact, anyone who has achieved true success in any field, has had a well defined plan with specific and realistically achievable goals. The process of developing and adhering to our goals gives us both long-term vision and short-term motivation. In fact setting goals helps us structure our time and stay focused which ultimately helps us attain the most out of our lives.

It's important to define our goals as clearly as possible, so we can witness our progress and accomplishments. Each personal success, no matter how small may not have been as easily recognized had we not defined our goals. The positive feedback from accomplishing our goals also tends to stem self defeating behaviour that could creep in and derail the progress that we had actually already made.

Winning isn't every-thing, but wanting to win is.

Vince Lombardi

By losing your goal, you have lost your way.

Friedrich Nietzsche

When actually setting our goals we must first create the big picture. That is what we ultimately want to achieve. Now don't let this be the first stumbling block. Most of us don't have any idea of our potential or where we really want to go. That's okay. The key is to just set a long-term goal. We can modify this goal as we better understand what we are really interested in and what we a capable of achieving. Secondly, we need to develop yearly, monthly, weekly and daily targets. For example, you want to attain and maintain your ideal body weight at 180 pounds, but you are currently at 204 pounds.

> *Success is the progressive realization of a worthy goal or ideal.*
>
> Earl Nightingale

This is a rough guideline for weight loss goal setting, but it spells out the general idea.

Long Term Goal: To weigh and maintain 180 pounds.
(To maintain 180 lbs one must eat approximately 3,500 calories per day and have a moderately active lifestyle.)

One Year Goal: Lose 24 pounds
One Month Goal: Lose 2 pounds per month
Weekly Goal: Lose ½ pound a week
Daily Goal: Reduce diet to 3,250 calories. (1,750 calories per week or ½ a pound)

(One pound of weight is equal to 3,500 calories)

When a person's goal is specifically spelled out, the task at hand doesn't seem so insurmountable. In fact the goal becomes quite attainable, so long as we maintain honesty and self-discipline throughout the year. That doesn't mean you have to be perfect, but if you go a little overboard one day you will need to make up for it on another day. Make a mantra of these three words: patiently, persistently and compassionately.

Success is the progressive realization of a worthy goal or ideal.

Earl Nightingale

For *Your Second Fifty* lifestyle program we will need to establish goals in all four dimensions: mentally, emotionally, physically and spiritually.

Mentally
Example: I will learn how to program and build a website.
Emotionally
Example: I will seek to understand before being understood.
Physically
Example: I will reduce my weight by ten pounds over the next year.
Spiritually
Example: I will work daily to develop a positive outlook on life.

It's very important to try to keep goals within reach to start. To aspire to win the Tour de France in the first year of cycling may be a bit of a stretch to say the least, but the biggest danger is that unattainable goals substantiate all the reasons why we shouldn't have even tried to do something in the first place.

The significance of a man is not in what he attains but in what he longs to attain.

Kahil Gibran

Another very important point is to make sure our goals honestly align with who we are and who we really want to be. If we don't like children, it wouldn't be advisable to return to college and study pre-school development.

Once we have determined our long-term and short-term goals, we need to review and up date them as needed. Keeping our ego in check here is of great importance - if we need to cut back a bit, we need to cut back; if we need to add a bit, we need to add. Easy does it and one-step at a time is the key to everything. Rome wasn't built in a day, nor will all these changes be easily accepted by the conscious and sub-conscious mind, but one-step at a time and easy does it will ultimately lead to attaining our goals.

If you want to be happy, set a goal that commands your thoughts, liberates your energy and inspires your hopes.

Andrew Carnegie

Do it now. You become successful the moment you start moving toward a worthwhile goal.

Author Unknown

If we feel we are failing or not succeeding at our goals, we need not worry. We simply need to keep moving forward and sooner than later, we will begin to notice a shift in our behaviours and attitudes. The process and states of mind we aspired to attain will follow suit shortly thereafter.

There is one quality which one must possess to win, and that is definiteness of purpose, the knowledge of what one wants, and a burning desire to possess it.

Napoleon Hill

Here are a few tips to consider when setting goals: when we write down goals we need to be positive; we need to eliminate any negative comments or words. We need to be precise by listing dates and the amounts or values that we intend to add or reduce. We also need to set our goals based upon performance and not the outcome. The outcome will naturally happen if we maintain our performance levels. Lastly, we need to determine our priorities and keep our daily goals within reach.

A goal properly set is halfway reached.

Abraham Lincoln

All-in-all setting goals helps us in all areas of our lives, from determining our priorities to eliminating many

> *There is no happiness except in the realization that we have accomplished something*
>
> Henry Ford

distractions and irrelevant intrusions. Once we establish our first goal our self-confidence will begin to rise and while there may be down days in the future, we will have taught ourselves that if we apply these newly acquired skills attaining our goals is only matter of time.

The Frank Experience - Goals

I had set goals a number of times in my life, but before 1989 I had never set definitive goals. Nor had I ever helped anyone else set and attain goals until the day I sat down with my sons and planned our trip to Disneyland.

This trip all came about because my oldest son Scott (6 years old at the time) had been talking to one of the Victoria, British Columbia's street musicians at a music festival, and during the conversation he had told Scott that if he and his brothers were to start busking in the inner harbor, they could make as much as $100.00 a day. Now I should explain that my sons were singing on telethons and at small music festivals at the time, and they were cute and actually quite good. (My other sons are Bob, Clint and Dave – triplets - and they were 5 years old at the time.)

So Scott came to me and asked if he could sing at the harbor. I have to admit I didn't like the idea because I didn't like the fact that I was going to look like I was exploiting my sons. So I said no. About a week later, when I arrived home, there was Scott walking out the door, guitar in hand, and heading to the inner harbor. (He would have been lucky to make it there by morning if he had walked.) I told him to come back in the house and we would talk about it after dinner, hoping he would forget all about it. I was back in college at the time, and after dinner the first book I opened was on entrepreneurship. Within seconds Scott was by my side and wanted to talk. What could I do? He wanted to be an entrepreneur. So I agreed to let him try on the following Saturday but only for one hour.

During that hour they made approximately $1,000.00, and the boys did nothing but talk about Disneyland all the way home on the bus. When we got home we all sat down at the table and began the process of setting targets and goals on a big sheet of cardboard.

First we had to figure out the costs of a trip to Disneyland, rent a van (we had no car), gas, hotels, tickets, and food. So I started making phone calls. The cost came to approximately $6,000.00, so we wrote that figure down. Then we needed to add 10% to give to charity (No specific reason; just the right thing to do. We would eventually donate the money to the David Foster Foundation in Victoria). That made the total cost about $6,600.00. Then we broke that number down over the 9 remaining weekends of the summer and realized that in order to make the trip, the guys would need to make $734.00 a week. To make a long story short, we left Victoria for Los Angeles the last week of August, and the boys even got to sing at Disneyland.

Currently, I have set new goals personally and financially, which I'm sure will come true, as all goals do. Unfortunately they usually take a little longer than I would have hoped.

Mental Dimension

Our mental dimension deals with our intellectual potentialities, or our capability to think things through. It is simply our ability to figure things out. Historically, the belief has been that our mental and intellectual capability deteriorates with age. However, research now shows that with proper stimulation, the brain not only maintains acceptable performance throughout its lifetime. In fact, it is capable of expansion and development.

"Intellectual growth should commence at birth and cease only at death"
Albert Einstein

In the past we were lead to believe that when brain cells died, the damage was permanent, and that the brain just deteriorated over time. However, more recent scientific research shows our brains may not only produce new brain cells or neurons throughout life, but the newly generated neurons quickly become involved in the formation of new memories.

Contrary to popular myth, you do not lose mass quantities of brains cells as you get older. "There isn't much difference between a 25-year old brain and a 75-year old brain," says Dr. Monte S. Buchsbaum, who has scanned a lot of brains as director of the Neuroscience PET Laboratory at Mount Sinai School of Medicine.

Contrary to past beliefs, scientific research now shows that IQ can be enhanced at any age with proper stimulation and that ones intelligence doesn't necessarily decline with age. The reason older people respond slower to questioning has more do with the fact that they are sifting through a life time of information than it does with diminishing mental capacities.

Scientists have now proven that the brain is plastic-like and that past views and perceptions of the brain's capabilities were somewhat off base. Researchers such as Michael M. Merzenich, a neuroscientist from UCSF, believes that the brain's plasticity can protect us from any physiological deterioration and overall decline in age.

The Nuns of Mankato

The brain's plasticity not only helps with recovery from injury but may actually play a role in preventing brain disease. For evidence, just visit the School Sisters of Notre Dame Nunnery in remote Mankato, Minnesota. Many are older than ninety and a surprising number reach one hundred; on average they live much longer than the general public. They also suffer far fewer, and milder, cases of Alzheimer's disease and other brain dementias. David Snowdon, the University of Kentucky professor who has been studying them for years, thinks he knows why.

Spurred on by their belief that "an idle mind is the devil's plaything," the nuns doggedly challenge themselves with vocabulary quizzes, puzzles, and debates about health care. They hold current-events seminars every week, and write often in their journals. Sister Marcella Zachman, featured in Life magazine in 1994, didn't stop teaching at the nunnery until she was ninety-seven. Sister Mary Esther Boor, also pictured in Life, still worked the front desk at ninety-nine. Snowdon, who has examined more than 100 brains donated at death by nuns in Mankato and other School Sisters locations across the United States, maintains that the axons and dendrites that usually shrink with age branch out and make new connections if there is enough intellectual stimulation.

John J. Ratey, M.D., is an associate professor of psychiatry at Harvard Medical School.

It's important to realize that the brain's capacity to function at a higher level is under our control and if we want to keep our brain functioning at a higher level, we need to continually challenge ourselves with new stimulating information. As the old adage goes, "use it or lose it".

Consider your brain a muscle, and find opportunities to flex it. "Read, read, read," says Dr. Amir Soas of Case Western Reserve University Medical School in Cleveland. Do crossword puzzles. Play Scrabble. Start a new hobby or learn to speak a foreign language. "Anything that stimulates the brain to think." Also, watch less television, because "your brain goes into neutral," he said.

In the book *Age-Proof Your Brain*, Tony Buzan's indicates that the very act of learning about your brain and educating yourself about the physiology and functioning of the brain in and of itself can stimulate and compel your mind to function at a much better level.

There are innumerable examples of people throughout history who possess great mental longevity. It has become a wonderful discovery that your brain has no limits in terms of its cognitive functioning, mental processing, intellect, and memory. The reality is that again you have control of all of these functions of your brain and your mind. So if you expect your memory to deteriorate and your mental prowess to decline with age, then your expectations will be fulfilled - this in and of itself is a self-fulfilling prophecy.

So if you expect to gain wisdom and have incredible mental capacity throughout your life into old age there is a high probability that this will happen to you. Remember it only takes ten years to become an expert, so if you are 90 years old you still have ten years before your Second Fifty is up.

It's also important to understand that the brain and body are connected and that we can enhance our mental capacity and cognitive processing with exercise and a healthy diet. Furthermore, by improving the functioning of our brain, our emotional state will improve, which in turn will facilitate positive change throughout all the dimensions. Thus, improving our mood, confidence, and self-esteem.

Exercise increases blood flow to the brain, releases hormones, stimulates the nervous system, and increases levels of morphine like substances found in the body (such as beta-endorphin) that can have a positive effect on mood. Exercise may trigger a neurophysiological high – by giving the body a shot of adrenaline or endorphins- that produces an antidepressant effect in some, an antianxiety effect in others, and a general sense of "feeling better" in most.

Michael H. Sacks, M.D.: Exercise For Stress Control

When we discuss emotions it's important to understand the role of the brain. Andrew Newberg in his book *Why God Won't Go Away* refers to the importance in differentiating between the terms "brain" and "mind." He defines the brain as a collection of physical structures that gather and process sensory, cognitive, and emotional data; whereas, the mind is the phenomenon of thoughts, memories, and emotions that arise from the perceptual processes of the brain. Without the brain's ability to process various types of input in highly sophisticated ways, the thoughts and feelings that constitute the mind would simply not exist. The brain cannot help but generate the thoughts and emotions that are the basic elements of our mind.

The mind has an incredible capacity to enter into altered states of consciousness, which may include mystical states and the ability to interpret spiritual experiences as real. It can therefore be concluded that all that is meaningful in human spirituality happens in the mind. Newberg states that studies show that electrical stimulation of the limbic structures in the brain produces gene-like hallucinations, out of body experiences and illusions, all of which occur during spiritual states. The area of the brain called the limbic system has sometimes been referred to as the "transmitter to God." The limbic system's most fundamental purpose is to generate and modulate primal emotions such as fear, aggressiveness, and rage. Other emotions like jealousy, pride, regret, embarrassment, and elation are all products of a highly developed limbic system, especially when its function is combined with the rest of the brain.

In addition recent research shows that the mind can actually regenerate and function after brain injury. Actor and director, Christopher Reeve, known for his performances as Superman, experienced what some call a "medical marvel." On May 27, 1995, Reeve had a serious horse riding accident. The accident left him paralysed below the neck and unable to breathe on his own. Experts predicted that Reeve would never breathe or regain the movement and feeling he had lost. In November 2000, doctor, John W. McDonald, M.D., Ph.D., watched in awe as Reeve slowly and deliberately raised the tip of his left index finger. McDonald believes that Reeve's case lays the foundation for additional studies examining the role of neural activity in regeneration and recovery of function.

The brain is an amazing organ and its functions don't need to deteriorate or decline as we age. Our brain/ mind has unlimited potential regardless of age. The key is to keep exercising it, challenging it, and to change our behaviour and beliefs with regard to our limitations and ability. Regardless of ones age, it is important to take risks and explore new avenues.

Since 1956, the Seattle Longitudinal Study has tracked more than 5,000 people, aged 20 to 90 years old. When participants began to experience cognitive decline, they were given a series of five one-hour training sessions designed to improve inductive reasoning and spatial orientation.

As a result, half of them improved cognitive functioning significantly – demonstrating that mental enrichment increases intelligence at any age. Lead researcher of the study, Dr. K. Warner Schaie, concluded: "The results of the cognitive training studies suggest that the decline in mental performance in many community-dwelling older people is probably due to disuse and is consequently reversible."

So how do we keep our minds sharp and positive? Simple, we exercise the brain. Now keep it real here, discard the belief "if you can't be number one, there ain't no point trying." This isn't about competing with physicists or Harvard scholars; it's about living and loving life one day at a time. All you need to do is challenge your mind daily. The mind is an amazing tool and the more we challenge it, the easier it becomes to address these challenges. Stick with it. Discipline is the key and you will have everything to gain. So play jigsaw puzzles, mind teasers, read a book - fiction or non-fiction makes no difference - learn to play an instrument, or challenge the mind to question because to questioning is the key to intellectual stimulation and growth.

For growth to happen we must remove our old ways of thinking and accept that our old beliefs may be flawed. The reality is we don't know half of what we think we know or even hope to know.

Your brain is the most powerful organ/instrument in your body. It has the capacity to create unbelievably wonderful experiences or moments of angst and depression. In fact your brain has the potential to completely change your whole life and your outlook on everything. The more you look the more you will find things that you enjoy. Again Rome wasn't built in a day, nor will we develop a completely new skill overnight. But to use a cliché "we reap what we sow," and the benefits harvested will be ours to enjoy throughout our second fifty.

Your First Five Emotional Footsteps

1) **Acceptance and Accountability** – So here we go, the first step! Acceptance and accountability. Do we challenge ourselves mentally? Do we read books that force us to think? Do we try to learn new things even if we have never done them before? Or are we of the mindset: "Well I did my time; I've done my part; I deserve to sit in front of a TV. I worked hard; I don't need to do anything!" Sorry maybe you do work hard, but that doesn't mean you should neglect or abuse your mind. If you're mentally slacking it, get back in the game.

2) **Establish Goals** – So what kind of goals are we looking at here? Maybe we decide to read a new book on a subject we have no previous knowledge. Or maybe we learn to play an instrument and dedicate four hours a week to practicing. Or may-

be we do the morning paper's crossword puzzle. It doesn't really matter what you choose, it only matters that you choose something that will force your mind to work. Something that will address new challenges and access areas of the mind that may or may not have been previously stimulated. But remember, you must challenge yourself and continually increase the level of difficulty.

3) **Experience Your Goals** – Here the old adage applies, use it or lose it. The mind can be compared to a muscle in that if it is not exercised it will shrink and become feeble.

    a. First, we need to understand that our minds are capable of addressing anything and everything. We just need to put in the time, look at things from different perspectives, and accept that some things just take a little more time than others.

    b. Second, we need to stay at it. We need to have the mindset, "I will get this done" and remove the all the unrealistic comparisons that we conjure up in our mind. The philosophy of one step at a time definitely works here.

    c. Third, we need to accept that there is no end goal here; we need to continue to learn something everyday of our life. Yes, you can learn something from TV, but TV watching is a passive activity, so while you are learning your brain isn't getting any stronger.

4) **Putting Our New Skill Into Practice** – It only takes ten years to become an expert so what the heck, become an expert at something. The interesting side to all of this is that learning does become easier the more we learn. When we learn, the

signals create a path through our brain. The more we learn the deeper engrained that path becomes and the more efficient our mind becomes at learning. A good example would be a game trail in the bush. The more animals that use a path the more established it is and the easier it is to walk on and use.

5) **Pass It On** – Most people like to hear something new and most people respect those with factual knowledge. Once those around you begin to recognize the keenness in your eyes and the sharpness of your mind, they will become interested in how you have been able to make these adjustments. Be willing to share your experiences. Everything done has twice the value of everything read. Remember, experience this book, don't just read it. In this book we only offer you a path; you must take all the steps including additional research on discipline, goals and all four dimensions. This in itself is a great way to fire up or stimulate your mental dimension.

The Frank Experience - Mental Dimension

Since turning fifty years of age, I have continually challenged my mental dimension by becoming a TESOL (Teachers of English to Speakers of Other Languages) certified English teacher, a TESOL trainer, a Director of Studies at an English academy, an A&R consultant in Thailand, an Expo coordinator, learning a second language, a communication tower installation representative and now an author. All of which I had to overcome my fear of the unknown and challenge myself to experience activities in which I had limited or no previous experience. At times the brain drain was intense.

But it was the book that I found most challenging. I'd developed the idea for this book "Your Second Fifty" for three years, but it wasn't until Mike said, "Why don't you just start writing. Write a little each day and before you know it the book will be done." So off I went, compiling and structuring the data for the Fifty Fantastic Days. All it took was to get the wheels in motion.

My original concept was to base the second fifty years around one's body, mind and soul, but Mike felt the book needed a fourth dimension: emotion. So we spent a weekend developing the structure of the book and decided to include sections on discipline and goal setting as well. Once the structure was in place I would compile all the pertinent information and write my first draft. For the first three sections Mike helped me with establishing an overall tone for the book and helped make sure that it conveyed the primary message. Once I had completed a section I would pass it over to Dale for a professional read and the final structuring.

Without question I'm sure that Dale's, Mike's, and my mental dimensions were challenged just by reading this book. However, in order to complete this book I needed to apply self discipline and to set challenging but attainable goals as well. The puzzle could not have been completed without applying all of the pieces.

I firmly believe that so long as I continue to challenge myself to overcome my fears, I will continue to expand my mental dimension, thus partaking in new activities and adventures throughout the second fifty years of my life.

Your Emotional Dimension

"...in navigating our lives, it is our fears and envies, our rages and depressions, our worries and anxieties that steer us day to day. Even the most academically brilliant among us are vulnerable to being undone by unruly emotions. The price we pay for emotional literacy is in failed marriages and troubled families, in stunted social and work lives, in deteriorating physical health and mental anguish..."

Daniel Goleman

The evidence has been piling up throughout history, and now neuroscientists have proved it's true: the brain's wiring emphatically relies on emotion over intellect in decision-making.

http://www.usatoday.com/tech/science/discoveries/2006-08-06-brain-study_x.htm

The world has become an increasingly difficult place to live. If we haven't the skills to maintain control over our emotions our lives will spiral out of control, and we will be stuck in the rut of casting blame either inward or outward.

Most people believe that emotions are caused by events. They are in fact caused by our interpretations of events, sometimes so fleeting and fast as to be beneath the level of consciousness. Our pre-conscious, split-second thoughts give rise to automatic emotional reactions. We then have a choice as to how we behave,

"Our beliefs create the world that we live in, and our beliefs and thoughts therefore also create the stress we experience. If we think something is safe and possible to conquer, then it is. But if we think the opposite then that will be our experiences.".

Janice Calnan, Psychotherapist

what we say, and how we handle a situation. The appropriateness of our actions and the effectiveness of our communications make up our emotional intelligence. People who are highly developed emotionally become sensitive to pre-conscious thoughts, questions their validity and appropriateness, and are able to directly influence their feelings, personal beliefs and behaviors.

Western culture has adopted the philosophy that it's all or nothing, 2nd place is unacceptable and can only be perceived as the 1st place loser. This unrealistic belief and expectation ultimately leads to criticism somewhere down the road and its fear of this criticism that leads to stress. What we need to understand is that stress can be addictive, and that this stress can have a direct result on the aging of our body and mind. We also need to understand that the event or situation that we believe caused the stress is not really the cause of the stress. Stress is created by your mental and emotional experience of the event or situation. This means you create your own stress. The good news is that with proper management of our emotions, we can reduce stress, which in turn reduces the additional wear and tear on our minds and bodies. As well researchers have concluded that people who deal effectively with others and exercise control over their own emotions are more likely to live happy lives.

So what can we do to improve our emotional control?

To start it would be a good idea to take an EQ (Emotional Quotient) test to understand your strengths and vulnerabilities. These tests are readily available on the Internet for a cost; however, if you purchase *The Emotional Intelligence Quick Book* by Travis Bradberry and Jean Greaves – an online EQ test is included with in the purchase price of the book.

Emotional Intelligence (EI) *= Understanding and Managing your Feelings and Emotions*
Emotional Quotient (EQ) *= Like IQ, a measure of one's emotional knowledge and understanding.*

With in the discussion of Emotional Intelligence there are many definitions and terms. However, for our purpose we will utilize the following as defined by Daniel Goleman:

Self-awareness - the ability to read one's emotions and recognize their impact while using gut feelings to guide decisions.

Self-management - involves controlling one's emotions and impulses and adapting to changing circumstances.

Social awareness - the ability to sense, understand, and react to other's emotions while comprehending social networks.

Relationship management - the ability to inspire, influence, and develop others while managing conflict.

Once we have an understanding of our strengths and vulnerabilities, we need to learn to identify the causes of our feelings and to become aware of our preconscious thoughts. We need to become aware because emotions are automatic responses to previously determined value judgments. Therefore, we need to carefully evaluate how we explained this situation to ourselves in the past and to proactively prepare for the next time this emotion arises. Here are a couple of examples: If we didn't have a belief that traffic should move quickly, then we wouldn't get angry when traffic slowed down. Traffic simply is what it is. It is our preconceived view of "how the traffic is supposed to move" that upsets us, not the traffic. Similarly, nobody makes us angry. We make ourselves angry by expecting people to act the way we want them to act and not accepting the way they really are.

The more aware we become of our emotions and associated reactions the better equipped we become at stemming and preventing situations that we may regret at some point later on in the future.

Valerie Cox's poem "The Cookie Thief" puts a unique twist on the dangers of impulsive emotional reactions.

The Cookie Thief

A woman was waiting at an airport one night,
With several long hours before her flight.
She hunted for a book in the airport shops.
Bought a bag of cookies and found a place to drop.

She was engrossed in her book but happened to see,
That the man sitting beside her, as bold as could be.
Grabbed a cookie or two from the bag in between,
Which she tried to ignore to avoid a scene.

So she munched the cookies and watched the clock,
As the gutsy cookie thief diminished her stock.
She was getting more irritated as the minutes ticked by,
Thinking, "If I wasn't so nice, I would blacken his eye."

With each cookie she took, he took one too,
When only one was left, she wondered what he would do.
With a smile on his face, and a nervous laugh,
He took the last cookie and broke it in half.

He offered her half, as he ate the other,
She snatched it from him and thought... oooh, brother.
This guy has some nerve and he's also rude,
Why he didn't even show any gratitude!

She had never known when she had been so galled,
And sighed with relief when her flight was called.
She gathered her belongings and headed to the gate,
Refusing to look back at the thieving ingrate.

She boarded the plane, and sank in her seat,
Then she sought her book, which was almost complete.
As she reached in her baggage, she gasped with surprise,
There was her bag of cookies, in front of her eyes.

If mine are here, she moaned in despair,
The others were his, and he tried to share.
Too late to apologize, she realized with grief,
That she was the rude one, the ingrate, the thief.

Valerie Cox

We also need to trust our natural instincts to understand what emotion it is that is arising at that given moment and be prepared to provide a positive response or better yet to just sit there and observe the emotion until it dissipates and passes.

The key to observing emotions as they arise is to understand and accept that emotions appear quickly and intensely. The emotion itself is only a sensation; it's us that needs to label it and give it direction and a life of its own. Once we master the skill of observation we will notice that when we become aware of the sensation rising, we don't need to react or respond because that sensation will fade just as quickly as it came.

Exercise and Emotion

In a recent study researchers have found that physical activity provides significant emotional benefits to people with personalities that tend to be more negative, anxious and depressed. Peter Giacobbi Jr., an assistant professor of sport and exercise psychology at the University of Florida's College of Health and Human Performance said, "We found that regardless of the events they experienced on any given day, they had an increased positive mood and a decreased negative mood on a day they exercised more. And that was pretty powerful."

Again it's developing and balancing our four dimensions that will lead us to a happy healthier life style.

James Blumenthal and a team of researchers at Duke University Medical Center found that an aerobic exercise program decreased depression and improved the cognitive abilities of middle-aged and elderly men and women. They followed 156 patients between the ages of 50 and 77 who had been diagnosed with major depressive disorder. They were randomly assigned to one of three groups: exercise, medication, or a combination of medication and exercise. The exercise group spent 30 minutes either riding a stationary bicycle or walking, or jogging three times a week. To the surprise of the researchers, after 16 weeks, all three groups showed statistically significant and identical improvement in standard measurements of depression.

Your First Five Emotional Footsteps

1) **Acceptance and Accountability** – This is the hardest step we will take in personal self-growth. In this

step we must be as honest as we possibly can be so that the path we lay out will lead us to where we really want to go. Here we need look in the mirror and state – "Do I have the courage to honestly begin to look at my strengths and vulnerabilities and am I ready and willing to begin this journey." First I will need to ask myself, just how much control do I have over my emotions? Do I have occasional outbursts or do I maintain calmness in the face of adversity?

Today more than ever we need to realise that getting things off our chest via emotional outbursts of any sort, won't accomplish what we've been lead to believe in the past. Venting our frustrations on others doesn't make us feel better; in fact, it usually makes us feel worse. The perfect example is getting cut off in traffic. We curse, display obscene gestures, and loathe the person possibly for hours, and does this make us feel better. Absolutely not. In fact all we've done is add additional stress and wear and tear to our bodies from our inability to control our emotions.

When we learn to control our emotions, we enhance our compassion and with greater compassion we are capable of considering possible alternatives as to why the person acted in the manor that they did. Once we consider these options we reduce the self serving anger that is associated in perceiving that the whole situation was in fact an act against us.

2) **Establish Goals** – Now we need to come to a clearer understanding as to what are our strengths and vulnerabilities. This is best understood after completing an EQ test. We suggest you look around and choose a test that you are comfortable in do-

ing – not only will this search give us a diversified perspective and more complete knowledge of EQ, but the process of searching will also be a positive stimulus for your mental dimension. Once you have completed the test you can then determine what areas of your EI (Emotional Intelligence) you want to focus on and improve.

3) **Experience Your Goals** – there is no short cut, there is no quick fix, and we must experience our goals one step at a time. This is where we apply our newly acquired skills of self-discipline.

    a. First, we need to observe the sensations that are happening in our bodies just prior to our emotional responses and reactions. Be patient as this will take time, if you are feeling impatient with your progress observe those sensations.

    b. Second, we need to observe the emotional responses and reactions that follow these sensations. Again this may take time, but soon enough patterns will begin to emerge.

    c. Third, we need to question ourselves to try and understand where and when it was in our life that we established our responses and reactions to specific sensations. For example, you dislike your brother's friend with the red hair and when he came over you always wanted to leave the house. Now as you are older, when you see a person with red hair, you have a strange sensation and then you feel the urge to leave.

    d. Fourth, we must be willing to question ourselves to see if our reaction is valid or if we may have established and based our response upon false or inaccurate information. Obviously, not all people with red hair pose a threat or warrant running from.

e. Fifth, we need to decide if the reaction is of a benefit to us or not. If our reaction isn't going to provide us with a positive result, it is best to just continue to observe it and let it dissolve and disappear. All emotions come and go relatively quickly, it's our behaviour and actions that give them life, validity, and reality.

Story of the two Monks

Two monks were making a pilgrimage. During the course of their journey, they came to a river where they met a beautiful young woman -- an apparently worldly creature, dressed in expensive finery and with her hair done up in the latest fashion. She was afraid of the current and afraid of ruining her lovely clothing, so asked the brothers if they might carry her across the river.

The younger and more exacting of the brothers was offended at the very idea and turned away with an attitude of disgust. The older brother didn't hesitate, and quickly picked the woman up on his shoulders, carried her across the river, and set her down on the other side. She thanked him and went on her way, and the brother waded back through the waters.

The monks resumed their walk, the older one in perfect equanimity and enjoying the beautiful countryside, while the younger one grew more and more brooding and distracted, so much so that he could keep his silence no longer and suddenly burst out, "Brother, we are taught to avoid contact with women, and there you were, not just touching a woman, but carrying her on your shoulders!"

The older monk looked at the younger with a loving smile and said, "Brother, I set her down on the other side of the river; you are still carrying her."

**The fight-or-flight response, also called hyperarousal or the acute stress response, was first described by Walter Cannon in 1915. His theory states that animals react to threats with a general discharge of the sympathetic nervous system, priming the animal for fighting or fleeing.*

http://en.wikipedia.org/wiki/Fight_or_flight

4) **Putting Our New Skill Into Practice** – The good news is that once we realise we have the ability to control our emotions, life begins to become more manageable. Our fight or flight behaviour* begins to subside and our acceptance of ourselves and others begins to increase. Self-destructive behaviour will of course attempt to re-establish itself; however, our new skills in addition to our goals and self-discipline will diminish the effect negative emotional reactions have over us. As we continue to question the validity of our responses, our compassion will begin to increase as we consider the other person's point of view. With increased compassion, comes peace of heart and greater happiness. A great meditation style for learning how to observe and deal with sensations and dealing with our emotions is Vipassana Meditation.

5) **Pass It On** – *Your Second Fifty* is a long term lifestyle shift and with today's society geared for the quick fix those of us willing to take up the challenge may appear to be walking a long and lonely path. However, once people begin to observe our emotional behaviour shift the laws of natural attraction will soon begin to take place. Other people's opinions will take on a new light and we will be interested in hearing them. Our need to be right will diminish, making us more appealing to others.

The key is to our emotional growth is awareness. We must remain aware of our emotions if we hope to control them, and once we do others will certainly be attracted to our new found happiness. Remember the old cliché "you can take a horse to water, but you can't make it drink," or when the student is ready the teacher will appear. The key is to tell everyone about the possibilities that lay before them and then let them decide for themselves. All we need to do is lead by example, and they will be certain to try sooner or later.

Happiness is never obtained in succeeding to be right – this is one of life's greatest illusions.
Frank Moffatt

The Frank Experience – Emotional Dimension

In my past I was always willing to argue or fight. I was aggressive and domineering and most certainly, I always needed to be right. Now I can say that while those emotions still arise from time to time, I can see them coming and prior to reacting, I now have an opportunity to disengage them. That doesn't mean I allow others to inflict their negativity or frustrations upon me, because I don't (or at least that to has be reduced), but now I try to deal from the truth and not my ego. Today I have a choice, I can provide a positive resolve or walk away, because conflict resolves nothing.

In 2004 I went on my first ten day silent meditational retreat and learned a great deal about my emotions. What I learned served me well for a couple of years but without self discipline and a support system to maintain consistent practice, I ended up slipping and falling back towards some of my old behavioral patterns.

It took a while to get back on track, but again I'm practicing and applying emotional awareness and control to my daily life. It was easier this time because of my previously established patterns and understanding.

I have since completed another ten day silent retreat and as to be expected from this type of practice, learned a great deal more about myself and just how limited my control is over anyone else and still at times over myself, but there is hope.

Well, I don't accept your insult, so it returns to you.

Buddha

I'm not a perfect person. However, each day that I attempt to maintain awareness of my emotions and work at enhancing my emotional intelligence, I have a much greater chance of not offending others. And so long as I don't accept another person's frustration, anger, or hate, what possible chance do they have of offending me?

Your Physical Dimension

It has been scientifically proven that there is nothing in the body that causes it to age. There are no time-released elements, or alarm clocks set to go off at specific times causing deterioration. The reason people age in appearance and attitude is because they believe they're supposed to. They've programmed themselves subconsciously to look and act a certain way at respective points in their lives.

They believe and accept age and therefore get old.

Jean Walters

Can you accept Jean Walter's comment? Do you have the courage to look outside of the box and admit that what you have come to believe may indeed not be the true? In fact do you have the willingness to consider that the way we may believe today may not even be the tip of our unlimited physical potential?

In the book "BioMarkers" by William Evans, Harvard Medical School has proved that the body completely rebuilds itself and can actually grow younger. So how long does it take your body to replace every cell in it? Seven years. In Deepak Chopra's book, Quantum Healing he states that our liver completely rebuilds itself every 6 weeks; our skeleton - every 3 months; our stomach lining - every 4 days and our skin - every month.

Physical fitness is not only finely interwoven with your intellectual, emotional, and spiritual dimensions, but plays an important role in maintaining overall well being.

A major five-year study at the Laval University in Sainte-Foy, Quebec of 5,000 men and women over age 65 who exercise regularly are less likely to show a decline in mental performance. On the other hand, those individuals who did not exercise and lived a more sedentary lifestyle were more likely to experience mental degenerative disorders.

In this section we will explore the physical dimension and the choices of healthy activities and alternatives that lay before us when considering our own person fitness programs.

We suggest that a fitness program provides a sensible balance between feeling good when one looks in the mirror and feeling good after one has participated in some form of exercise or activity. Keep in mind physically fit bodies take time to develop. If we focus on the end result of our goal the task will appear insurmountable, but if we go about it one day at a time, before one knows it we will have enough improvement to have a new appreciation for our physical self. Take it easy – have fun.

Here are a few tips to consider when exercising.

Exercise for YOU! Don't subject yourself to self-professing experts. Everyone has an opinion and while his or her intent may be honorable, spare yourself from his or her kindness. If you really need help to develop a program seek out a professional trainer at your local gym or internet directory. At the end of this section we will provide you with a number of options that will hopefully assist you in your search for expanded awareness and understanding of your Physical Dimension.

The word exercise derives from a Latin root meaning "to maintain, to keep, to ward off." To exercise means to practice, put into action, train, perform, use, and improve.

Go about things slowly and trust your body to let you know what is right and what is not right for you. But how will you know if what you are doing is right? We did say go about it slowly didn't we? Trust yourself, follow the instructions for whatever exercise you have chosen (a number of exercises are listed near the back of this book) and take it easy.

Listen to your body, it will tell you if the movement feels acceptable and if the weight or resistance is safe. Again if you're not comfortable trusting yourself seek out a professional until you have developed enough confidence to trust yourself. In any case only you will know if you are being honest with yourself and once that honesty has been developed, trust will soon follow.

The National Institute on Aging states that osteoporosis is a preventable disorder when weight-bearing exercises such as "walking, jogging, playing tennis and dancing," become lifestyle activities done three to four times per week.

Keep active! Working out and cardiovascular exercise are non-negotiable options when it comes to improving and maintaining physical health. Resistance training (weight training) needs to be based on an increased resistance program, so the body will have an opportunity to maintain or even gain bone density and muscle mass. That being said, one needs to be patient and increase resistance slowly. Nothing puts a bigger dent into the start of a new workout program than an injury and all the self-defeating behavior that accompanies it.

Aging Well, NY State

Not long ago, it was "accepted knowledge" that older people could not increase their muscle strength nor their muscle mass. Now, happily, this myth has been dispelled. In 1989, researchers from Tufts and Harvard Universities undertook a study of older people in their late 80's and 90's. They did three sets composed of eight weight lifting repetitions each for three days a week.

After two weeks, they were retested and the weights were increased. At the end of six weeks, these frail older people had increased their muscle strength on average by 180 percent. What is more interesting, none of the participants had reached a plateau. As a result of their increased muscle strength, their average walking speed increased 48 percent. Two participants no longer needed their canes, and one participant was able to rise from a chair without using the chair arms.

All of the participants resumed their sedentary lifestyles at the end of the program. The researchers then retested them, and found a 32 percent loss in maximum strength after only 4 weeks without training. The moral of this story is "If you don't use it, you'll lose it." But the happy ending is that you can regain your fitness and strength at almost any age which will help you to retain or regain your independence, freedom, and add to your good looks.

http://agingwell.state.ny.us/fitness/index.htm

Balance and stretching exercises also play a key role in maintaining the physical component of ones life. A great way to accomplish both goals would be to attend yoga classes a couple of times a week. Again remember, Rome wasn't built in a day. Go about your program one-day at a time and before you know it you'll be pleasantly surprised with your newly acquired flexibility and balance.

An additional benefit to improved overall balance is the reduced fear of falling.

"People have the mistaken idea that exercise is a fabulous way to lose weight," says William Evans of the University of Arkansas for Medical Sciences. "But exercising doesn't burn a lot of calories." Walking or running a mile burns about 100 calories. But sitting still for the same time burns about 50 or 60 calories. "So the extra you expend isn't huge and people get discouraged at their slow rate of weight loss."

You don't need a day off. I repeat: you don't need a day off. Stay active and live life to the fullest. The only people that benefit from a sedentary society are furniture salesmen and convenience stores. You gain nothing from being a couch potato. You don't deserve any of the self-inflicted diseases associated with lethargic behavior. Keep this in mind: as human beings we are innately lazy, that's just the way it is. Therefore, we must take the initiative to make things happen. We will never be free in life until we take full responsibility and ownership of our lives.

So the first step in taking responsibility is to build ourselves a weekly workout routine.

Workout Routine Example (Expanded Examples are located in Appendex A)

Monday: Aerobics (brisk walk for thirty minutes or yoga)
Tuesday: Resistance Training (chest, back & shoulders)
Wednesday: Aerobics (water aerobics)
Thursday: Resistance Training (Legs, arms and abdominal)
Friday: Aerobics (Tennis, Badminton or yoga)
Saturday: Resistance Training (chest, back & shoulders)
Sunday : A walk in the park, gardening, or mall shopping

Following Week (Switch things up a bit)

Tuesday: Resistance Training (Legs, arms and abdominal)
Thursday: Resistance Training (chest, back & shoulders)
Saturday:Resistance Training (Legs, arms and abdominal)

Whatever, program you choose to develop for yourself will be the right program, so long as you take it easy to start and pay attention to your body and what it is telling you. As you gain experience with exercising you will make adjustments based upon the new information you have attained. There is no right and wrong in choosing exercises so long as you follow the proper steps for each exercise. One fact remains: it is always healthier to do something than to do nothing at all.

A Healthy, Well-balanced Diet

The first thing you need to know is what your body needs nutritionally. The key to achieving and maintaining nutritional health is knowing what, when, and how much to eat.

Choices should be:

- Of a moderate calorie content, nutrient-dense: low in fat and sodium and high in fiber and calcium.

- Tasty so you enjoy them.
- Easy to chew, swallow, and digest.
- Easy to make.
- Pleasing to look at.

Stay away from processed foods and stick to natural food products by:

- **Focusing on good carbohydrates.** Choose whole grain (brown rice, whole wheat bread, rolled oats, barley, millet); stay away from "white" products, such as white rice, white bread and products made with white flour.
- **Eating raw fruits and vegetables.** Try to eat at least two daily serving of your fruits and vegetables raw, as this will help to preserves their nutritional value. If you wish to cook your vegetables steaming is best as it preserves the nutrients.
- **Keeping the protein lean.** Fish, poultry, eggs, beans, peas, nuts, and tofu are all healthy sources of protein. To bake, broil, grill, steam, or poach your meal will help you maintain a healthy, low-fat, low cholesterol diet.
- **Consuming calcium.** Milk, cheese, and yogurt are all excellent sources of calcium, whereas cream cheese, cream, and butter are not. If possible purchase fat-free or low fat dairy products.
- **Choosing healthy fats.** Olive oil and sunflower oil, avocados and avocado oil, nuts and seeds are all great.
- **Hydrating your body.** A suitable allowance of **water** for adults is 2.5 litres **daily** in most instances. In addition to drinking water, consumption of high water content foods such as melons, grapes,

cucumbers, onions and apples help to keep us properly hydrated and flush toxins from the body, while keeping our joints flexible and our minds clear.

- **So now that you have read the list and you're saying, "where is the beef and where is the bacon?"** Well again that's up to you. Moderation is the key to healthy living. No one is saying you shouldn't have a piece of chocolate cake at your son's birthday or a nice thick juicy steak at the family reunion. A calorie is a calorie so indulging every now and then certainly won't be worth the grief or guilt many of us have grown accustom to heaping on ourselves when we slip up a bit.

The key is actually to become aware of what, when, and where we are eating at all times. Too often we find ourselves eating, not because we are hungry, but because we are trying to suppress another emotion that is stirring inside. Food fuels our body like gasoline fuels our car, put in the wrong grade and your car will ping as you drive down the road. So think about it, you can either ping or purr through life and that choice is 100% up too you.

Calories in One Pound of Body Weight

It takes about 3,500 calories to make 1 pound. This pertains to whether they are food calories coming in, or calories (burned by exercise) going out. If you eat 3,500 calories more than your body needs, you will gain about 1 pound. If you use up 3,500 calories more than you eat, you will lose about 1 pound.

Calories Needed Per Day

Here is a simple formula to use as an estimate for your daily calorie requirements:

- ❖ Change your weight from pounds to kilograms: Divided total pounds by 2.2
- ❖ The average persons basal metabolic rate is approximately 1 calorie per kilogram per hour. Multiply your weight in kilograms by the 24 hours in a day. You will burn this many calories just staying alive.
- ❖ Now factor in your additional daily calorie consumption based upon your activity level:
  - Light activity: 50% to 70%
  - Moderate: 65% to 80%
  - Heavy: 90% to 120%
- ❖ If you have a desk job and workout 30 minutes per day, this would be considered light activity. Most N. Americans fit into this class.
- ❖ If your job involves physical activity and you are physically active in addition to your workout (walk to work, use the stairs, etc.), this would be moderate.
- ❖ Construction workers, athletes, etc. would be considered heavy activity.
- ❖ Once you have calculated your basic calories needed to stay alive, add them to your activity calories and you will have an approximation as to the number of calories you need per day.

Example:

Say you weigh 180 pounds. Divide by 2.2 to get 81.81 kilograms. (Round down or up as required if you wish) 81.81 times 24 hours = 1963.63 calories needed per day for basic function.

Let's say you're activity is light:

1963.63 times 50% = 2945.44 (2945)

963.63 times 70% = 3338.17 (3338)

So for a person weighing 180 pounds that is lightly active, they would burn between 2945 to 3338 calories per day. To lose weight, you need to burn more calories than you eat, by either eating less or exercising more.

One Potentially Dangerous Fast Food Day:

Breakfast	Bran Muffin 5oz	405
	Orange Juice 1 cup	100
Lunch	Hamburger	500
	French Fries	500
	Coca Cola – 12oz/ 375 ml can	200
Dinner	Large Taco	500
	Tortilla chips, taco, 8oz	1,100
	Cookies & Cream (Haagen-Dazs) ½ cup	270
Evening	Beer (3)	315
	Pretzels, 8oz	900
Total Calorie Intake		**4,790**

This would equal nearly a 1/2 of a pound gain for a 180-pound man, whose daily activity was light.

The best indicator for your healthy weight range is the Body Mass Index (BMI). The BMI is a measure of body fat based on height and weight that applies to both adult men and women. You can find BMI tables on the internet.

For those of you that consider yourself big boned - sorry - there is no scientific data to substantiate that big bones have any significant affect on ones overall weight classification or BMI.

Mental Road Blocks

Everything that we do in our lives is linked mentally, emotionally, physically, and spiritually. So even if we were to follow the greatest workout program ever designed and strictly follow the ultimate diet, our physical gains may still fall short of our expectations if we don't have a positive physical image of ourselves. And why might that be you ask? Perhaps it is that we don't believe we are worth it.

It's a scientifically-proven fact that our mind doesn't know the difference between what's real and what's imagined. So the good news is that we have the ability to change our self-image and our external image to anything we want, provided it falls in line with who we really are. In fact anything we focus our thoughts on the mind will start the process of creating it. That is unless we have a stronger negative view from our emotional self that overrides this process. That negativity could be based upon a fear attached to our projected image; it could be that our image is not in agreement with whom we really are; or it could be based on the values of others; or the guilt based "I should". If there is any conflict between your desired self and your internal self-image, your goals may be quite difficult to attain. BUT not impossible!

Positive self-imaging that is in line with who we really are has the potential to erase this conflict. Remember, negative thoughts lead to negative results and positive thoughts lead to the positive possibility of change and a newly enhanced self-image.

Thus, self-imaging is developed by the mind, ignited by emotions, incorporated into the body, and inspired by faith. So once we have consciously developed the image of who we want to be, we add the other elements to bring our image into a four dimensional reality. Hence, we become our image.

Once we've reached this level of actualization, we must maintain our new self-image, by confronting and resolving any behaviours or patterns that challenge our new image of ourselves. Certainly there will be challenges and disillusionment along the way as there is in any endeavour; however, be assured these are only momentary set backs and you will bounce back on track and inline with your newly acquired self-image. Things always get really bad before they turn the corner to reward and success. It's those that persevere that reap the rewards and those that quit and procrastinate say it doesn't work.

Stress

With an improved self-image, comes an enhanced awareness of how to deal with life's daily challenges and stresses. However until that awareness of your new self image is firmly entrenched one needs to be aware of the effects of stress on weight control and management. When we are stressed we can gain weight even if we haven't increased the amount of food we are consuming. When we are stressed we naturally produce cortisol. Too much cortisol slows the metabolism, resulting in a weight gain that totally confuses the people affected.

When we experience chronic stress we tend to crave more fatty, salty, and sugary foods, which includes sweets and processed foods. The fat we store when stressed tends to be stored as abdominal fat, which presents greater health risks than fat stored on the other parts of our body.

Alternative Fitness Options

Fitness comes in many forms and not only from lifting weights, running, swimming and riding a bike. Keep your eyes and ears open. Everyday something new will pop up and before you say nay give it a try, because until we try something, until we experience something we really have no idea what the heck we are talking about.

Massage

There are a numerous massage therapy techniques available to gently nurture your body.

- **Swedish Massage** – utilizes tapping and kneading strokes to work the entire body to relieve muscle tension and loosen sore joints.
- **Thai massage** – utilizes various stretches and acupressure points to increase flexibility, release muscle tension and energy blocks.
- **Deep Tissue Massage** – utilizes slow strokes and direct pressure or friction movements that go across the grain of the muscles to relieve chronic tension.
- **Rolfing** - utilizes hands and elbows to realign and straighten the body by working the myofascia, the connective tissue surrounding your muscles and holding your body together.

An increasing number of research studies show massage reduces heart rate, lowers blood pressure, increases blood circulation and lymph flow, relaxes muscles, improves range of motion, and increases endorphins (enhancing medical treatment). Although therapeutic massage does not increase muscle strength, it can stimulate weak, inactive muscles and, thus, partially compensate for the lack of exercise and inactivity resulting from illness or injury.

It also can hasten and lead to a more complete recovery from exercise or injury.

www.holisticonline.com

Yoga

Born in India, almost 26,000 years ago, yoga presents an excellent alternative in which to develop ones spiritual, mental, and physical dimensions.

The four main yoga's are:

- ❖ **Karma Yoga:** Selfless Work
- ❖ **Bhakti Yoga:** Love and Devotion
- ❖ **Jnana Yoga:** Knowledge and Discernment
- ❖ **Raja Yoga (or Ashtanga Yoga):** Meditation

Yoga Classes

If you are considering joining a yoga class we would recommend, Hatha yoga, or a beginners Iyengar class. Hatha yoga is very focused and allows you to become fully aware of each pose. Hatha and Iyengar yoga's are very well suited for physical and mental health as well as those with disabilities and or injuries.

Bikram or "hot yoga" is performed in a room heated to 37 degrees Celsius. (This temperature may be hard for some people to handle.) Bikram yoga is derivative from Hatha yoga. The order of the asanas (poses) is important, and the sequence always stays the same. In Bikram yoga the focus is on health and fitness.

Yoga, an ancient but perfect science, deals with the evolution of humanity. This evolution includes all aspects of one's being, from bodily health to self-realization. Yoga means union

- the union of body with consciousness and consciousness with the soul. Yoga cultivates the ways of maintaining a balanced attitude in day-to-day life and endows skill in the performance of one's actions.

~B.K.S. Iyengar, Astadala Yogamala

Your First Five Physical Footsteps

1) **Acceptance and Accountability** – Your first physical step should be either on to a scale or in front of a full size mirror "NAKED". Now are we happy? Certainly not if we are comparing ourselves with all the airbrushed models on today's magazines. So, it's time to get realistic, we don't need to be sex goddesses, we need to be healthy. If we are fat, we are fat. If we eat unhealthy foods, we are unhealthy. Again what is: is. If we are over weight and unhealthy we need to accept it and we need to shed all the excuses as to why we are the way we are. Accept and be accountable.

2) **Establish Goals** – What is it we really want? Are our everyday tasks a burden? Do we have aches and pains that we would love to be rid of? Do we feel sluggish and uninspired? All of these hassles and pains can be greatly reduced by exercise. So let's get started. We need a balanced program to include cardio, strength and stretching exercises. One hour a day five days a week is plenty. In fact a 20-20-20 minute program is ideal to start.

   To build your program, look at the exercises at the back of the book and try and do one exercise per body part per workout. Remember this is fitness training for overall health – not completive training for bodybuilding or to run in a marathon. It would be a good idea to write down your specific goals, whatever they may be. Take it easy to start, we don't want to give ourselves an excuse to quit right off of the top and if you have had health issues in the past or are unsure about your health, it would be wise to consult a doctor prior to exercising.

3) **Experience Your Goals** – You can read all you want about fitness, eat all the supplements in the world, but if you don't live the experience there is no possible way to reap the rewards.

   a. First, you need to organize the exercises you have chosen for that day onto a list. You need to leave room so you can add the weights you chose in the next step. This will help keep things flowing smooth each time you train. Do Cardio first, strength second, and stretching third.

   b. Second, you need to test the weights to ensure that what you will be lifting isn't too heavy. Start at the lightest and work up until you find a weight that is comfortable. Again this isn't about ego; you don't need to impress anyone. You need to improve your health. As time goes on set little monthly goals to increase the weights you are lifting.

   c. Third, you need to complete your workout each day and try to do all the exercises you have chosen within the prescribed time. When you are working out keep moving as this keeps your body parts warmed up and reduces the risk of injury. You can chat and socialize after you finish training.

   d. Fourth, on your day or days off still stay active, take a walk, climb stairs do anything but sit on a couch and within a couple of weeks you may not see a difference but you will certainly begin to feel and notice a difference.

4) **Putting Our New Skill Into Practice** – By establishing a new workout routine, you will be replacing one of your old sedentary routines. This in itself will add vigour and confidence to your life. However you need to be aware of one potential danger. That being the belief that now that you are exercising you can increase your calorie intake. Sorry but this belief is not true. While exercise does burn more calories than if you are sedentary, the amount you burn really isn't that much more. If you are looking to loose weight, the only effective way is to reduce your calorie intake.

   Remember the saying beauty is only skin deep? Well exercise goes a lot deeper and you can't always see the benefits of your actions. A healthy life is within your grasp, all you need to do is put in the effort. If it's not working be honest and revisit what you are doing – maybe the intensity needs to be stepped up and the chatting reduced.

5) **Pass It On** – Once you have established a consistent workout program and you are relatively consistent in attendance, you might want to share what you have experienced with your friends, so they too can overcome some of their pains and aches. Of course it's nice to have a training partner, and a husband or wife can fit that bill nicely. In fact it's a great way to spend an hour together. Once the physical change catches up to the internal changes you won't have too hard of a time convincing your friends to give it a try. Just remember easy does it and one step at a time. Attract rather than promote.

The Frank Experience – Physical Dimension

In my fiftieth year my first big challenge was the *Body for Life Program* - a brutally tough twelve week program that required me to train six days a week, one hour a day.

The first step of the program was to set my goals, and man did I set them. I couldn't tell you the last time I was at 10% body fat but it was something I really wanted, so I wrote it down. For my bench press I had made a 240lb lift for 4 reps when I was about 34, so a 250lb lift didn't appear completely out of reach. Nor was a 350lb squat out of the question, as I had done 300lbs for 4 reps also at 34 years of age.

Once the goals were in place I went about my business of showing up everyday and disciplining myself to stick with the program.

My first goal was to drop 11% body fat , from 21% to 10%. **Made it!**

My second goal, bench press 250lbs for 6 reps – max to start was 180lbs. **Made it!**

My third goal, to squat 350lbs for 6 reps – max to start was 200lbs. **Made it!**

So did it work? Yes! Would I recommend this program? Not necessarily. I was so tired and wore out at the end I stopped exercising and over ate gaining back 10 pounds in the first two weeks. Now I enjoy more of an active lifestyle that keeps the aches and pains at bay. But if you want to give a strenuous training program a shot, by all means feel free. After all only you know what's best for you.

Today I walk everywhere I can, time permitting, and I like to lift weights three times a week. I'm just starting out at yoga and twice a week seems to be working out for now; however, I can see myself giving it a shot three times a week in the near future - once I can bend a little more. As for my intensity to live life to the fullest, I always intend to do my best, (key word - intend - I don't always succeed, because as a fellow human I also fall prey to my innately lazy tendencies). Overall however, my competitive nature is waning, and for that I'm happy. My competitive ego hasn't been all that great of a friend to me in the past anyway.

Your Spiritual Dimension

Spirituality, in its most narrow sense, pertains itself to matters of the spirit. Spirituality is often associated with non-physical, eternal perceptions of humankind's ultimate nature, a sense of connection with something greater than oneself. A faith or belief, which may or may not include some form of emotional experience of a religious nature.

To accomplish great things, we must not only act, but also dream; not only plan, but also believe.

Anatole France

Often spiritual traditions, share a common theme: the path, practice, or tradition of understanding one's true meaning and the relationship one has with the rest of existence, a higher power, and the universe or life.

The word spirituality tends to conger up its fair share of controversy. However, what we believe to be important is not whom you consider to be your higher power, but only that you are willing to open your mind and consider that there may be some power or force of nature that has and will continue working with you when formulating and attaining your goals and dreams.

Once you are willing to place your faith in a higher

There are no mistakes, no coincidences. All events are blessings given to us to learn from.

Elisabeth Kubler-Ross

power whatever that be God, Buddha, Allah, or Mother Nature, you will be able to tap into your spiritualist dimension, which allows you access to and to accept miracles as they unfold in your daily life.

Upon acceptance of our spirituality, conscious awareness becomes an ever-increasing part of our lives and with that awareness comes acceptance to life as life unfolds. When we accept life as it is we can make adjustments that are appropriate, effective and realistic. Self-discipline becomes more prevalent and we become more aware of our responsibilities and our power of choice.

Meditation

Meditation is not about religious or philosophical beliefs. Meditation is about conscious awareness. When practicing meditation our intellectual beliefs become trivial. In meditation we seek to access our inner reality. To go beyond our conscious awareness and all the information others have told and to access the wisdom of the ages.

With expanded conscious awareness we begin to live in the "now," we begin to experience life minute-by-minute, moment-by-moment – we actually begin to live. Eckhart Tolle has written a fascinating book called *The Power of Now* and in his book he describes the benefits of living in the now. Below is a little introduction taken from his website.

Most people are ill at ease and restless because they are all the time bewildered by the constant inflow of thoughts in their mind. They can't stop thinking. There is no inner peace and calm. They give the impression of being haunted by something. Their emotions give rise to new thoughts and their thoughts give rise to new emotions. So they are fettered to this vicious chain of cause and effect. This is what makes them so unhappy, because they seem not to be able to let loose of their thoughts and enjoy the happiness of the Here and Now. All the time their thoughts take them adrift.

For the mind creates the past and the future. If we would have no thoughts we would be forever living in the happiness of an Eternal Now. But instead, our thoughts force us to be mesmerized by our past, both with guilt and with feelings of nostalgia, and also by the future, the outcome of which is always too uncertain and too fickle to make it worth a second thought, one would say; but nevertheless people go on thinking and worrying, which are in most cases synonymous, about the future.

Out of fear for the Void behind our thoughts we keep clinging to the content of our mind. We can not let our thoughts be for what they are, mere bubbles in a vast ocean, but we are so used to identifying our self with mind, that our whole notion of self is derived from it. We just give our mind too much credit and what is worse: we think we are having these thoughts, while it would be more accurate to say that Consciousness is having these thoughts in this particular mind in this particular body.

So in order to be happy we have to learn to disidentify with our thoughts and emotions and take a higher stance in witnessing our internal life. That way we shall develop presence in the Here and Now and learn not to be taken away anymore.

Eckhart Tolle - http://home.wxs.nl/~brouw724/EckhartTolle.html

> *Having spent the better part of my life trying either to relive the past or experience the future before it arrives, I have come to believe that in between these two extremes is peace.*
>
> Author Unknown

Spiritual power is one's ability to still make decisions with greater and greater awareness. Spiritual power resides within us. Spiritual power is wisdom, or the ability to make decisions with maximum awareness and to consider the ramifications of our actions before we make them. To be aware of these consequences is consciousness and to be conscious ultimately means to accept life on life's terms. What is, is.

Awakening

An "awakening" is a moment of clarity in which a new insight or understanding is gained. With this new awareness the experience of life is seen differently, and new possibilities are opened. Changes in patterns of thought, emotions, and behavior occur. An awakening allows the possibility of growth to new levels of psychological and spiritual maturity.

lessons4living.com

It's the non-acceptance of what is, is, that retards spiritual growth. This non-acceptance is in actuality an avoidance of accepting and dealing with pain, which we experience when facing our fears, the unknown, and situations that don't favour us. To avoid these fears we apply subconscious defences; we actually block or discard unpleasant facts from our awareness thus limiting our conscious awareness. To overcome these defences and fully realize and embrace our potentialities we must find the courage to accept life as it is presented to us and to accept the pain and suffering that is a necessary component of our growth. What this all boils down to is that in order to solve our problems we must solve our problems. We must honestly accept them, address them, and deal with them.

Once we commit to honestly dealing with our pain and suffering we are well on our way. Of course no one is perfect and slips will happen; however, over time our internal paradigm will begin to shift and we will be more effectively able to accept and deal with our fears.

At times this process may appear as though we are taking one step forward and two steps back. However, nothing in life of any value comes easy. That being said, everything we do to enhance any of our four dimensions will pay dividends throughout our remaining years.

Ways to Developing Our Spiritual Dimension

Meditation

Meditation allows one to still the mind and allow new insight to enter into one's life.

- Set 20 to 30 minutes aside each day – this is a great way to start your day off on a positive note.
- Find a quiet place to sit where you won't be disturbed. It's not important to sit in the lotus position; a comfortable chair will be fine. Dress comfortably.
- It's best to set an alarm so that you won't have to worry about time.
- Focus on your breath. Breathe naturally.
- Focus on your breathing and nose area. When you notice thoughts entering your mind gently move them out of your consciousness and refocus on your breathing.
- When your time is up slowly open your eyes, take a few deep breaths, and stand up slowly.

Most people have trouble letting go of the Western world's tendency to think, think think. To think is only to rehash old information. Be patient; a turbulent mind will take time to be tamed.

Meditative techniques play an important role in the Arthritis Self-Help Course at Stanford University. Fifteen to twenty percent of the more than 100,000 people with arthritis that took the 12-hour course and learned the meditation-style relaxation exercises reported a reduction in pain.

A strong link has also been established between the practice of Transcendental Meditation and longevity. Only two factors have been scientifically determined to actually extend life: caloric restriction and lowering of the body's core temperature. Meditation has been shown to lower core body temperature.

http://www.1stholistic.com

Yin and *Yang* Therapy Balls

Therapy balls are made of various metals and can be painted in a multitude of designs and colors. The balls are delicately weighted and at times may encompass soothing chimes. According to traditional Chinese beliefs, our vital organs are all connected to the fingers. By rotating these balls in one hand it is believed that this action stimulates the circulation of blood and energy throughout the body.

Prayer

Prayer is the act of attempting to communicate, commonly with a sequence of words, with a deity or spirit for the purpose of worshiping, requesting guidance, requesting assistance, confessing sins, or to express one's thoughts and emotions. The words of the prayer may take the form of a hymm, incantation, or a spontaneous utterance in the praying person's words.

Wikipedia

For decades the medical community basically ignored he impact of religion on health. But in recent years, scientists have begun studying the possibility that faith matters. "There are hundreds and hundreds of studies — scientific studies — that show that religious people are healthier."

Dr. Harold Koenig, Duke University's Center for Spirituality, Theology and Health.

Prayer can be a very effective way to relieve oneself of stress and anxiety. When we pray we surrender control over a situation and ask for help. The act of asking for help opens the door and allows the universe to assist us. The challenge is to keep an open mind and the awareness to see the answers to our prayers, as they may not resemble exactly what we had asked for.

St. Frances Prayer

Lord, make me an instrument of thy peace!
That where there is hatred, I may bring love.
Where there is wrong, I may bring the spirit of forgiveness.
That where there is discord, I may bring harmony.
That where there is error, I may bring truth.
That where there is doubt, I may bring faith.
That where there is despair, I may bring hope.
That where there are shadows, I may bring light.
That where there is sadness, I may bring joy.
Lord, grant that I may seek rather to comfort, than to be comforted.
To understand, than to be understood.
To love, than to be loved.
For it is by self-forgetting that one finds.
It is by forgiving that one is forgiven.

There are two sayings that have the potential to lead us to miracles, (Faith Can Move Mountains and No Prayer Goes Unanswered) yet there are those of us who are still reluctant and skeptical to believe. But why? What possible harm can come of us if we exercise faith? By exercising faith all things are possible, without faith we are limited, limited to our perceived limitations.

A father walked into his son's room while the little boy was praying. "Son, why do you pray?
Praying is a waste of time." The little boy looked up and said "God answers my prayers."
The father shook his head and said, "There is no God, you are wasting your time."
The little boy again looked up at his Dad and said, "There is a God and he answers my prayers."
The father shot back, "Oh really, well you've been praying for a new bike for over a year now
and I don't see any bike out there, so tell me how did God answer that prayer."
The little boy smiled and said, "Not yet."

Everything in life has its time and place. We as humans tend focus on our immediate needs and wants, limiting our view on life as a whole. However the more we practice our spirituality, the more positive our approach is to life's daily challenges, trials, and tribulations and we begin to see life as it truly is, amazing and abundant.

Your First Five Spiritual Footsteps

1) **Acceptance and Accountability** – How could we ever believe in something we cannot see? Well there's always electricity or oxygen. We don't dispute their existence and we can't see them either. So why do so many of us dispute spiritually and

the existence of a higher power? Probably because our ego doesn't like the competition, our egos want us to believe we are the masters of our own destiny, that we are our own Gods. In part this belief is true, but like thinking (rehashing ours or others old thoughts) why would we want to limit ourselves when the rewards are so amazing? Every day we are presented with countless miracles that we blow off as coincidences or the norm. Most often, because we are too stressed or going way too fast to ever notice. The key is to open our minds to the endless possibilities that are presented to us daily. Miracles are happening every moment. It is our acceptance of a higher power and the coinciding gift of humility that allows us to see and reap the benefits of these miracles. In life what we give we get. So if we want happiness and peace we need to be sure that's what we are putting out there.

2) **Establish Goals** – When we develop goals in our spiritual dimension it is very important that we have a greater plan in mind. It's one thing to set a goal to make a million dollars; it's a completely different thing to set a goal to make a million dollars with the intent of helping others while helping yourself. When we are thinking spirituality our limits are endless as to what we may set for goals. This is the dimension where miracles are designed and manifested. In this dimension we need to understand that everything is possible. Positive belief and faith returns positive results, negative beliefs return negative results. So if you set no limits upon your thoughts – you in turn set no limits upon your reality.

Physical Reality is a Manifestation of Thoughts

They have demonstrated what the "New Science" has been pointing to for nearly half a century: that our universe is more like a thought than a thing and is actually a manifestation of consciousness. While this will be one of science's most life-changing revelations ever, for many it will not be a new notion ... just as the spherical nature of the earth and the sun's central place in our universe were not new ideas once they were finally accepted by the masses.

The truth of the creative nature of thought has also been around for a very long time. Mostly, it's been known in the domain of religion and spirituality - "As ye believe, so shall it be," "We reap what we sow." However, in 2004, filmmaker and entrepreneur William Arntz brought these ideas - and their scientific underpinnings - to millions more through his groundbreaking, award-winning, hybrid documentary feature film, What the BLEEP Do We Know!? The film explored the emerging convergence of these ancient spiritual principles with leading edge science. And pointed out how adherence to these new notions of reality will utterly change the planet.

By Thomas Herold in Scientific Background on March 2nd, 2007
www.dreammanifesto.com

3) **Experience Your Goals** – Again, there are no short cuts in attaining our spiritual goals. Spiritual growth comes with spiritual practice. If we stick to it we will soon realize just how much more positive our life is becoming.

    a. First, we need to ensure that we really believe in what we want to attain. That our goal meets with our core beliefs of ourself. Who we really are and what we really want to do.

    b. Second, we need to let go of our goal. If the goal is of a worthy cause it will now manifest itself all by itself. It is our job to go about the daily business of living our lives in the now.

c. Third, we need to be aware of the signposts that are presented to us as we embark upon this journey. Through our increased awareness our higher power provides the guidance, but it's up us to get the job done.

During a terrible flood a man was seen hanging out of his 2nd story window by two would be rescuers in a boat. "Quick jump in the boat!" one of the rescuers cried. "It's OK, God will save me." The man replied. A couple of hours passed and the water continued to rise. The man had now climbed on the roof and was spotted by a rescue helicopter. "Quick grab the rope!" the pilot called out over the P.A. system. "It's OK, God will save me." The man replied. A couple of hours passed and to the man's surprise the man found himself standing at the gates of heaven. He looked up at God and said, "Why didn't you save me?" God replied, "Who do you think sent the boat and the helicopter?"

4) **Putting Our New Skill Into Practice** – Discipline, discipline, and more discipline. Sorry but again nothing of any value comes easy in life and meditation and prayer take time to master.

   First let's look at meditation. Meditation takes time to reach a point where it becomes productive and when we are able to quell our monkey minds (The endless battle that rages between our ears engaging the past and our perceived future.) It is very important that we be patient with ourselves, and that we try and be as consistent as possible when and where we practice. Remember we don't need to be perfect; we just need to give this new skill set a fair chance. In fact it may be a good idea to take in a mediation workshop, because effort ill spent won't produce the results we are looking for and may derail our entire mindset and belief.

When we address prayer, we are referring to prayer as sending out a positive message into the universe with the intent of making the world a better place. So when we pray it only makes sense to send love through pray for others. If we have faith we don't need to pray for ourselves; our higher power has that all under control. We just need to live the old saying "what we give, we will receive in return."

5) **Pass It On** – As our manifestations become reality, those closest to us will witness our shift in attitude and demeanour. Keep in mind that throughout our spiritual journey more will be revealed to us daily on a need to know basis. Again the key is to share what we have experienced, not what we have read. We only want to put it out there for others, so they can decide for themselves if this is what they want. When people are ready to learn their teacher will appear all we can do is plant the seed.

The Frank Experience – Spiritual Dimension

I've been blessed with a number of truly amazing experiences in my life; however, none more impressive or enlightening than the one that happened about twelve years ago in Nashville, Tennessee.

Five years after my sons' eventful summer of singing on the Victoria causeway, they found themselves signing a major label recording contract with Polydor Records in Nashville. While living in Nashville we would take the opportunity to, once a month, sing at the children's hospital.

During one of those visits after the boys had performed, I asked the hospital's PR representative if there were any shut-ins and could we possibly go to their room and sing them a song or two. After checking she said that there were indeed a couple of kids we could visit. After singing to the two children we were walking down the hall on our way out of the hospital, and I noticed a little girl about three or four years old lying in a bed.

I asked the nurse if we could sing for her and she said she didn't think it was a good idea because the little girl only had a couple of weeks left to live. As I have said before, my emotional control wanes at the best of times, so I proceeded to say with a somewhat challenging tone, "Well, ask the mom?" The nurse refused, and my voice began to rise as I said, "If she only has two weeks left why do you want to prevent her from experiencing something so positive and uplifting?" Just then the doctor walked by and asked what the problem was? I explained that I thought that the nurse should ask the mother if the boys could sing for her daughter. The doctor responded by saying, "Let me ask." Thankfully, the mother invited us in. The boys introduced themselves to this frail little girl and proceeded to sing a song on their album that Garth Brooks had written: "When God Made You." Everyone broke into tears. Then the boys sang a little ditty that Clint (one of the triplets) and I had written called: "With a Little Smile." Upon the completion of that song everyone was back to smiling. As we were leaving the room, I realized I had one of the boy's CD's with me, so I went back and asked the little girl if she would like it. She nodded and I gave it to her. I then told her that we were going out on the road to sing but if she was here when we got back in four weeks, I would give her the boy's other CD.

When we got back off of the road, I had the record label book us another show at the hospital. After the show we walked down to her ward to see if she was still there, CD in hand. We had just opened the doors to the ward and the head nurse came over to us and said, "She's been asking for that CD every day since you guys left."

She had made it past the two weeks, so I came up with another idea. I told her that in two months the boys would be doing a show with Toby Keith in downtown Nashville and that if she could get strong enough to leave the hospital, I would get her front row tickets to the concert. Two months later she was sitting front row. After that show we headed out to Las Vegas and didn't get back until November. When we returned to Nashville, we had the record label again schedule a show at the hospital, and after the show we went straight to her ward. When we got there the nurse we spoke to said she was gone. Our hearts all dropped, and she then realized what she had said and corrected herself saying, "No, no she's gone home."

After that we moved to Las Vegas, Nevada, and then to Branson, Missouri, and then spent five years touring the world. We never saw that little girl again, but we learned a very valuable lesson – she believed, when others didn't, and she survived. She is a miracle.

Everyday we are all witnesses to miracles, some small some incredible. I've learned to accept them for what they are and not try to intellectualize them away. Now

I work at accepting life as it unfolds each day. I've taken my turn at playing God in my life, (challenging others to do things my way, because I knew what was best for them) but to be honest I didn't do a very good job of it. So from here on out, I think I'll try and follow my higher power's queue and respect others to make their own best decisions and choices for them selves, but when I slip up I hope I have the awareness to hear people when they kindly refuse my unsolicited advice.

When we look for love and acceptance from another being it is only to fill the void and emptiness we have failed to fulfil within ourselves.

Frank Moffatt

Conclusion

So now it's up to you. We've opened the door and shown you the path. What you make of it will depend 100% upon your willingness to overcome your previous beliefs and behaviours.

The challenge here is to live your second fifty years of your life one day at a time and to the best of your ability. Once you set your dimensional targets, change will begin and over time evolution and progress is certain to happen. Remember you are human and error and slips are just a part of life. Be kind to yourself, forgive yourself, and then get back at it – everything is just a matter of practice, time, and effort.

Again, this isn't about coming in first, it isn't about being better than someone else, and it isn't about the final destination. This is all about the journey, all about enjoying life to its fullest, all about accepting the cards that are dealt to us, and all about making positive adjustments that lead to positive personal growth and change. There are no time limits.

If before putting this book into action you could remember one person's name in ten and after a month of expanding and working on your mental dimension you were able to remember two names out of ten, that's progress. The key to personal growth in all of the dimensions is not to compare ourselves with others or the expectations of others but to see our improvements and to be proud of them, no matter how small or how insignificant they may appear.

I wrote this book with hopes to stimulate your interests in all four dimensions of your life and with the desire that you would then make positive changes. Research, explore, and experience whatever it is that will ignite your passion within. Your second fifty years can be and should be both rewarding and productive.

At times western culture tends to disregard the value of wisdom that only comes with age. So never underestimate your value to future generations and all the wonderful benefits that they will reap from your discipline and dedication in living your second fifty years to the fullest of your potential.

In life we do not have the right to complain or blame. If we complain or blame we are not being accountable and responsible for our current state of affairs. Once we become accountable and responsible we receive the right to all that is ours to avail and enjoy – happiness, love, and freedom.

Frank Moffatt

Fifty Fantastic Days

Health & Happiness

With any exercise program, seniors should see a doctor and obtain clearance prior to beginning the program.

Spiritual Quote

Truth, like surgery, may hurt, but it cures.

Han Suyin

Quote of the Day

Do not believe in anything simply because you have heard it.

Do not believe in anything simply because it is spoken and rumoured by many.

Do not believe in anything simply because it is found written in your religious books.

Do not believe in anything merely on the authority of your teachers and elders.

Do not believe in traditions because they have been handed down for many generations.

But after observation and analysis, when you find that anything agrees with reason and is conducive to the good and benefit of one and all, then accept it and live up to it.

Buddha

Fascinating Food Facts

You cannot loose weight using a Low Fat Diet. Low fat foods have been popular for more than 15 years, but yet or society is getting more overweight as each year passes. This fact should tell you that eating a low fat menu is not the answer to losing weight.

Mind Massage

What's filled in the morning and emptied at night, and one day of the year its emptied in the morning and emptied at night?

Emotional

In a book called The Fifth Discipline (by Peter M. Senge), Senge quotes an article called "Advanced Maturity," by B. O'Brien: "Whatever the reasons, we do not pursue emotional development with the same intensity with which we pursue physical and intellectual development. This is all the more unfortunate because full emotional development offers the greatest degree of leverage in attaining our full potential."

Fitness Facts

Begin your exercise program at a relatively moderate level of intensity, progressing gradually to safely allow your body the time to adapt to the program.

Spiritual Quote

Wisdom is not a question of learning facts with the mind; it can only be acquired through perfection of living.

N. Sri Ram

Quote of the Day

When your work speaks for itself, don't interrupt.

Henry J. Kaiser

Food Facts

Carrots really do help prevent blindness. Vitamin A is known to prevent "night blindness," and carrots are loaded with Vitamin A.

Mind Massage

A bus driver was going down a street. He was on the wrong side. He went past a stop sign. He didn't signal at a turn. He went under the minimum speed and yet he didn't get in trouble for his actions.

Why not?

Emotion

The key to success is to keep growing in all areas of life - mental, emotional, spiritual, as well as physical.

Julius Erving

Fitness Facts

Just because you have begun to exercise doesn't mean you can over eat during your day. If you consume more calories than you burn off in a day, you will gain weight. The key is a balanced diet and exercise plan.

Spiritual Quote

There can be no happiness if the things we believe in are different from the things we do.

Freya Madeline Stark

Quote of the Day

To be 70 years young is sometimes far more cheerful and hopeful than to be 40 years old.

Oliver Wendell Holmes

Food Facts

Fast food eaters can become chemically dependent on the fat and sugar found in fast food. Scientists say these substances affect the same areas of the brain as people with drug addiction.

Mind Massage

What are the next two letters in the following sequence?

E, O, E, R, E, X, ?

Emotion

Awfulizing: The belief that a situation is more than 100% worse than it is

Catastrophizin: making mountains out of mole hills

John W. Maag

Fitness Facts

Physical activity builds physical vitality. With every year of your life, you have more to gain from being physically active.

Spiritual Quotes

People only see what they are prepared to see.

Ralph Waldo Emerson

Quote of the Day

Dignity consists not in possessing honours, but in the consciousness that we deserve them.

Aristotle

Food Facts

Hens with white feathers and white ear lobes produce white-shelled eggs and hens with red feathers and red earlobes produce brown eggs; the colour has no relationship to the nutritional quality or taste of the eggs.

Mind Massage

A man is at a river with a 9-gallon bucket and a 4-gallon bucket. He needs exactly 6 gallons of water.

How can he use both buckets to get exactly 6 gallons of water?

Note that he cannot estimate by dumping some of the water out of the 9-gallon bucket or the 4-gallon bucket.

Emotion

We can't solve problems by using the same kind of thinking we used when we created them.

Albert Einstein

Fitness Facts

Crunches and other abdominal exercises can help you strengthen your abdominal muscles and improve your posture and abdominal muscle tone. But muscle is muscle and fat is fat. If you want a more athletic waist, you need to lose the fat to show off your abdominal muscles.

Spiritual Quotes

Success isn't permanent, and failure isn't fatal.

Mike Ditka

Quote of the Day

It's never too late to be who you might have been.

George Eliot

Food Facts

In 1295 when Marco Polo returned from China to his homeland of Italy, he brought back a recipe for "Milk Ice." Europeans substituted cream for the milk and the dessert favourite ice-cream was born.

Mind Massage

Recently, Snow White's seven dwarfs met up with three of their friends and went to the cinema to see Bambi. From the clues below, can you determine the order in which they stood in the ticket queue?

Grumpy was in front of Dopey. Stumpy was behind Sneezy and Doc. Doc was in front of Droopy and Happy. Sleepy was behind Stumpy, Smelly, and Happy. Happy was in front of Sleepy, Smelly, and Bashful. Bashful was behind Smelly, Droopy, and Sleepy. Sneezy was in front of Dopey. Smelly was in front of Grumpy, Stumpy, and Sneezy. Dopey was in front of Droopy. Sleepy was in front of Grumpy and Bashful. Dopey was behind Sneezy, Doc, and Sleepy. Stumpy was in front of Dopey. Smelly was behind Doc.

Emotion

Most people don't realize that it is the meaning they assign to people and events that actually generates emotions. Commonly used statements such as "He made me mad." "She made me sad." or "That really made me happy." not only reflect this mistaken belief but actually reinforces it.

Fitness Facts

Exercise can slow down, halt, and possibly even reverse many aging trends. Much of the decline that is commonly associated with the aging process is often the result of lifelong inactivity and improper lifestyle habits. Research clearly demonstrates that if an active lifestyle is maintained into later years, a relatively high level of function may be retained and vigorous activity can be engaged in both safely and successfully.

Spiritual Quotes

Begin at once to live, and count each separate day as a separate life.

Seneca

Quote of the Day

Use what talents you possess: the woods would be very silent if no birds sang there except those that sang best.

Henry Van Dyke

Food Facts

A North American Indian named George Crum invented potato crisps.

Mind Massage

What does this say: merepeat

Emotion

Painful as it may be, a significant emotional event can be the catalyst for choosing a direction that serves us - and those around us - more effectively. Look for the learning.

Louisa May Alcott

Fitness Facts

Weight lifting helps maintain adequate muscular strength, endurance, and tone as well as promoting joint mobility and increased flexibility.

Spiritual Quotes

I learned that we can do anything, but we can't do everything…at least not at the same time. So think of your priorities not in terms of what activities you do, but when you do them. Timing is everything.

Dan Millman

Quote of the Day

Life is like a rose; you can lie upon the pedals or become entangled amongst the thorns.

Frank Moffatt

Food Facts

Almonds are a member of the peach family.

Mind Massage

There is a family party consisting of two fathers, two mothers, two sons, one father-in-law, one mother-in-law, one daughter-in-law, one grandfather, one grandmother, and one grandson.

What is the minimum number of persons required so that this is possible?

Emotion

Controlling ones emotions through Doc Lew Childre's Freeze Frame technique.

1) Recognize your stressful feelings and make the decision to freeze-frame (call a time-out).

2) Shift your focus away from your racing thoughts and emotions.

3) Think about a fun time in your life; a time in which you felt positive.

4) Ask your heart for a more efficient and effective response to the situation you are freeze-framing.

5) Open yourself up and listen to the answer your heart gives you.

Fitness Facts

Eating a low-salt, reduced fat, diet with plenty of fruits, vegetables, and fibre can actually reduce your age-related risks of heart disease, diabetes, stroke, osteoporosis, and other chronic diseases.

Spiritual Quotes

To be wise is to live in an inner harmony that eventually overcomes all outer discords.

N. Sri Ram

Quote of the Day

We all have the extraordinary coded within us, waiting to be released.

Jean Houston

Food Facts

Chewing gum stimulates signals in the learning centre of the brain and thus helps save memory as you age.

Mind Massage

How many letters are in the alphabet?

Emotion

In Emotional Intelligence, Daniel Goleman describes the five major components: Component 1 - Knowing one's emotions. Self-awareness — recognizing a feeling as it happens — is the keystone of emotional intelligence.... [T]he ability to monitor feelings from moment to moment is crucial to psychological insight and self-understanding. An inability to notice our true feelings leaves us at their mercy. People with greater certainty about their feelings are better pilots of their lives, having a surer sense of how they really feel about personal decisions from whom to marry to what job to take.

Day # 9

Fitness Facts

No matter how poor your current level of fitness, you can start an exercise routine and become fitter and healthier at any age.

Spiritual Quotes

The Vietnamese are our brothers; the Russians are our brothers; the Chinese are our brothers and one day we've got to sit down together at the table of brotherhood.

Martin Luther King, Jr.

Quote of the Day

... happiness gives us the energy which is the basis of health.

Henri-Frederic Amiel

Food Facts

Corn Flakes are about 8% corn.

Mind Massage

This engulfing thing is strange indeed, the greater it grows the less you see. What is it?

Emotion

In Emotional Intelligence, Daniel Goleman describes the five major components: Component 2 - Managing emotions. Handling feelings so they are appropriate is an ability that builds on self-awareness.... People who are poor in [the ability to soothe oneself, to shake off rampant anxiety, gloom, or irritability] are constantly battling feelings of distress, while those who excel in it can bounce back far more quickly from life's setbacks and upsets.

Fitness Facts

About 25 percent of North American adults - and an even greater percentage of women - are sedentary. After age 44, upwards of 30 percent of women are sedentary, and by age 65, the proportion increases to almost 35 percent. By the time they reach age 75, about 50 percent of all women are sedentary.

Spiritual Quotes

Be kind, for everyone you meet is fighting a hard battle.

Plato

Quote of the Day

Happiness is not a station you arrive at, but a manner of traveling.

Margaret Lee Runbeck

Food Facts

Fortune cookies are not from China; they were invented in Los Angeles around 1920.

Mind Massage

A certain street has 1000 buildings. A sign-maker is contracted to number the houses from 1 to 1000. How many zeros will he need?

Emotion

In Emotional Intelligence, Daniel Goleman describes the five major components: Component 3 - Motivating oneself. Marshalling emotions in the service of a goal is essential for paying attention, for self-motivation and mastery, and for creativity. Emotional self-control — delaying gratification and stifling impulsiveness — underlies accomplishment of every sort. And being able to get into the "flow" state enables outstanding performance of all kinds. People who have this skill tend to be more highly productive and effective in whatever they undertake.

Fitness Facts

In addition to its many positive physical benefits, regular exercise can develop self-awareness of the body and improved mental well-being.

Spiritual Quotes

Wanting to reform the world without discovering one's true self is like trying to cover the world with leather to avoid the pain of walking on stones and thorns. It is much simpler to wear shoes.

Ramana Maharshi

Quote of the Day

A man should not leave this earth with unfinished business. He should live each day as if it was a pre-flight check. He should ask each morning, am I ready to lift-off?

Diane Frolov and Andrew Schneider

Food Facts

Fish consumption may be more than just brain food because it also helps to protect your eyes from age-related macular degeneration, which is a potential cause of blindness.

Mind Massage

One barrel of pickles weighs 60 kgs, while one box of mangoes weighs 18 kgs. What is the weight of one crate of cherries and one sack of potatoes, when the sack of potatoes and the box of mangoes together weigh as much as the barrel of pickles and the crate of cherries?

Note that two crates of cherries weigh as much as one box of mangoes.

Emotion

In Emotional Intelligence, Daniel Goleman describes the five major components: Component 4 - Recognizing emotions in others. Empathy, another ability that builds on emotional self-awareness, is the fundamental "people skill." People who are empathic are more attuned to the subtle social signals that indicate what others need or want. This makes them better at callings such as the caring professions, teaching, sales, and management.

Fitness Facts

Men who exercise regularly are less likely to have problems with erectile dysfunction than are men who don't exercise, especially as they get older.

Spiritual Quote

The bond that links your true family is not one of blood, but of respect and joy in each other's life.

Richard Bach

Quote of the Day

When a friend is in trouble, don't annoy him by asking if there is any thing you can do. Think up something appropriate and do it.

Edgar Watson Howe

Food Facts

Mayonnaise will kill lice and also condition your hair.

Mind Massage

There is a one-floor house, and everything in it is blue, green or purple. The people are purple, the carpeting is green, and the walls are blue.

What colour do you suppose the stairs are?

Emotion

In Emotional Intelligence, Daniel Goleman describes the five major components: Component 5 -The art of relationships is, in large part, a skill in managing emotions in others. ...These are the abilities that undergird popularity, leadership, and interpersonal effectiveness. People who excel in these skills do well at anything that relies on interacting smoothly with others; they are social stars."

Fitness Facts

Heart disease, stroke, diabetes, osteoporosis, and cancer are all believed to be exacerbated by your lifestyle.

Spirituality

For every sin but the killing of time there is forgiveness.

Sufism

Quote of the Day

He who is drowned is not troubled by the rain.

Chinese Proverb

Food Facts

Heinz Catsup leaves the bottle traveling at 40 kilometres per year.

Mind Massage

A woman has 7 children, half of them are girls.

How can this be possible?

Emotion

The greater the feeling of inferiority that has been experienced, the more powerful is the urge to conquest and the more violent the emotional agitation.

Alfred Adler

Fitness Facts

Older adults require exercise as much as younger individuals; however, the benefits for seniors are even more pronounced.

Spiritual Quotes

If you and I are having a single thought of violence or hatred against anyone in the world at this moment, we are contributing to the wounding of the world.

Deepak Chopra

Quote of the Day

It is no use to blame the looking glass if your face is awry.

Nikolai Gogol

Food Facts

Pizza originated in the early 1700's in Naples, Italy.

Mind Massage

Mr. Smith lives at 20, Rose Street with his wife Debi. They have nine sons and each son has one sister.

How many members are in Mr. Smith's family?

Emotion

Demandingness: The use of the words "should/shouldn't," "have to," "need to," and "must." These words represent a magical way to change reality to the way we want it.

John W. Maag

Day # 15

Fitness Facts

Following your exercise sessions, if you don't allow the muscles adequate time to recover, you may run the risk of over training and possible injury.

Spiritual Quotes

All of us have the capacity to attract to ourselves what seems to be missing in our lives.

Dr. Wayne Dyer

Quote of the Day

When you cease to make a contribution, you begin to die.

Eleanor Roosevelt

Food Facts

Milk is the new diet drink since low-fat, high-calcium dairy foods may burn off fat since extra calcium increases metabolism.

Mind Massage

A person travels on a bicycle from home to church on a straight road with wind against him. He took 4 hours to reach there. On the way back to the home, he took 3 hours to reach as wind was in the same direction. If there is no wind, how much time does he take to travel from home to church?

Emotion

Once you learn and accept that emotional responses are preceded by automatic thoughts, it becomes easy to teach yourself how to focus your attention on them during the heat of the moment. Once this happens you will see for yourself that these thoughts and images appear between the events and our emotional responses.

Fitness Facts

Moderate activity that lasts less than an hour may reduce your appetite for an additional hour or two, while intense exercise of an hour or more may increase appetite.

Spiritual Quotes

What we think, we become.

Buddha

Quote of the Day

One's dignity may be assaulted, vandalized and cruelly mocked, but cannot be taken away unless it is surrendered.

Michael J. Fox

Food Facts

Puffed grain was invented by Alexander Anderson in 1902. Unlike popcorn, a type of corn that naturally pops or puffs up with heat, puffed cereal or snacks are formed by exploding whole grain kernels under high pressure and steam.

Mind Massage

A boy goes into a shop to buy some sweets. He uses a $1 coin and buys 40 cents worth of sweets. The shop assistant gives him two coins for his change.

One of them was not a 50-cent piece, so how could the boy have gotten his exact change?

Emotion

Many people believe that they are powerless; that it is external circumstances that hold the power over them; that their life is simply a series or reactions against or responses to the circumstances that they encounter. In order to regain power, a person needs to believe that he or she can make choices independent of the circumstances.

Fitness Facts

Muscle will never turn into fat. Muscle is muscle and fat is fat. They are two separate types of tissue.

Spiritual Quotes

The danger is that every religion, including the Catholic one, says "I have the ultimate truth." Then you start to rely on the priest, the mullah, the rabbi, or whoever, to be responsible for your acts. In fact, you are the only one who is responsible.

Paulo Coelho

Quote of the Day

Health is not valued till sickness comes.

Dr. Thomas Fuller

Food Facts

Strawberries are the only fruit which has its seeds on its outer skin.

Mind Massages

Five horses ran in the race.
There were no ties.
Whisper did not come first.
Lightning was neither first nor last.
Eclipse Glory came in one place after Whisper.
Thunder was not second.
Sunshine was two places below Thunder.
In what order did the horses finish?

Emotion

Essi Systems of San Francisco has found that only factor which does have a significant impact on a person's ability to handle stress — particularly work pressure — is personal power; i.e., control over your time, resources, information, and other elements connected with work. Says Esther Orioli, the founder of Essi Systems, "Our testing revealed that out of 21 stress-related factors we examined, personal power was the only factor that could predict who got sick and who stayed healthy in work situations with high amounts of pressure. Conversely, people without this sense of personal power tended to feel victimized and were unable to cope with high amounts of pressure in similar situations."

Fitness Facts

Simply adding movement into your daily routine can increase your level of fitness. Take the stairs, park so you are forced to walk, even taking the dog for a walk all counts. Try and keep tabs so that you put in 30 minutes of exercise a day.

Spiritual Quotes

The more you have, the more you are occupied, the less you give.

Mother Teresa

Quote of the Day

I don't know the key to success, but the key to failure is trying to please everybody.

Bill Cosby

Food Facts

Popsicles were invented by an 11 year old, Frank Epperson, when he left a stirring stick in his soda water drink overnight on his porch.

Mind Massage

You have two jars, 50 red marbles and 50 blue marbles. A jar will be picked at random, and then a marble will be picked from the jar. You can place maximum of 50 marbles in each jar.

Placing all of the marbles in the jars, how can you maximize the chances of a red marble being picked? What are the exact odds of getting a red marble using your scheme?

Emotion

Just as physical fitness exercises strengthen the body, one can strengthen ones Emotional Fitness through daily meditation and deep breathing exercises. The exercises will help strengthen your ability to deal with life's daily stresses and pains.

Day # 19

Fitness Facts

Taking higher amounts vitamins and supplements will not enhance you physical goals.

Spiritual Quotes

Even as the fingers of the two hands are equal, so are human beings equal to one another. No one has any right, nor any preference to claim over another.

Muhammad

Quote of the Day

Youth is a disease from which we all recover.

Dorothy Fulheim

Food Facts

Peanuts are one of the ingredients in dynamite.

Mind Massage

There was a crime scene at this house where a man lies dead slumped over his desk. There was a note next to him that said to push the play button. When the cops arrived they pushed it and a voice said, "My life is too complicated and I can't take it any more." Then there was a gunshot.

How did the cops know that this was a murder?

Emotional

One of the most critical aspects of gaining more emotional control is to learn how to identify your automatic thoughts. In most instances, our negative emotional responses are directly preceded by automatic thoughts. These automatic thoughts remain hidden for most of us. Unless you train yourself to look for these thoughts, you will probably not be aware of them. But once you do learn how to catch hold of your automatic thoughts, you will not only become aware of them, but you also learn how to control them.

Day # 20

Fitness Facts

Only take salt tablets under a doctor's supervision. You will never sweat enough during regular exercise to require additional salt.

Spiritual Quote

Love one another.

Jesus of Nazareth

Quote of the Day

Where there is an open mind, there will always be a frontier.

Charles F. Kettering

Food Facts

White chocolate is not a true chocolate because it contains no chocolate; instead, it's made of sugar, cocoa butter, milk solids, lecithin, and vanilla.

Mind Massage

What row of numbers comes next?

This is a tough one!

1

11

21

1211

111221

312211

13112221

Emotion

Curiosity doesn't matter any more. These days people don't want to be transported to emotional territories where they don't know how to react.

Hector Babenko

Fitness Facts

The more physical activity you engage in, the more time you should devote to flexibility & stretching work.

Spiritual Quotes

The will is a product of integrity, not a child of contradictions.

N. Sri Ram

Quote of the Day

One hundred percent of the shots you don't take don't go in.

Wayne Gretzky

Food Facts

Rice paper does not contain one grain of rice - it's made from either Rice straw, Bamboo, Hemp, Mulberry leaves, Wingceltis, or Gampi.

Mind Massage

In Mr. Powell's family, there are one grandfather, one grandmother, two fathers, two mothers, one father-in-law, one mother-in-law, four children, three grandchildren, one brother, two sisters, two sons, two daughters, and one daughter-in-law.

How many members are there in Mr. Powell's family? Give minimal possible answer.

Emotion

I-can't-stand-it: imagining one can't tolerate situations or have any happiness if the situation persists.

John W. Maag

Fitness Facts

Exercise helps elevate your mood and keeps depression at bay.

Spiritual Quotes

Three things in human life are important. The first is to be kind. The second is to be kind. And the third is to be kind.

Henry James

Quote of the Day

The battles that count aren't the ones for gold medals. The struggles within yourself - the invisible, inevitable battles inside all of us - that's where it's at.

Jesse Owens

Food Facts

Vegemite is an Australian icon, which was developed in 1922 by Dr. Cyril Callister. He took used brewer's yeast and blended the yeast extract with ingredients like celery, onion, salt, and a few secret ingredients to make this paste rich in B vitamins; it was developed for the Fred Walker Company, which is now Kraft Foods.

Mind Massage

When Alexander the Great attacked the forces of Porus, the Greeks captured an Indian soldier. He had displayed such bravery in battle, however, that the enemy offered to let him choose how he wanted to be killed. They told him, "If you tell a lie, you will be put to the sword, and if you tell the truth you will be hanged."

The soldier could make only one statement. He made that statement and went free. What did he say?

Emotion

Think about any attachments that are depleting your emotional reserves. Consider letting them go.

Oprah Winfrey

Fitness Facts

Lifestyle physical activity, such as taking the stairs, gardening, and walking instead of driving, is as effective as structured gym workouts in improving fitness.

Spiritual Quotes

If you judge people, you have no time to love them.

Mother Teresa

Quote of the Day

Nothing will ever be attempted if all possible objections must be overcome first.

Anonymous

Food Facts

Ten gallon hats only hold about 6 pints or 2.8 Litres.

Mind Massage

What is round as a dishpan, deep as a tub, and still the oceans couldn't fill it up?

Emotion

By taking control of our emotions and minimizing the degree to which we indulge in negative emotions (and all negative emotions are basically a form of self-indulgence), we not only increase our personal freedom, but we also become vastly more effective and efficient human beings.

Day # 24

Fitness Facts

Improving fitness appears to help men live longer following a heart attack.

Spiritual Quote

Believe nothing, no matter where you read it, or who said it, no matter if I have said it, unless it agrees with your own reason and your own common sense.

Buddha

Quote of the Day

Courage is going from failure to failure without losing enthusiasm.

Winston Churchill

Food Facts

Tea strengthens bones because isoflavonoid chemicals in tea may have a weak estrogenic effect, reducing bone deterioration and osteoporosis risk.

Mind Massage

A state has a law stating that no man or woman can marry more then once within that state. There is a man that legally marries more than 10 times in that same state.

Who is that man?

Emotion

My house is my refuge, an emotional piece of architecture, not a cold piece of convenience.

Luis Barragan

Fitness Facts

When you improve your strength and stamina, it's easier to accomplish everyday tasks like carrying the groceries and climbing the stairs.

Spiritual Quote

Happiness cannot be traveled to, owned, earned, worn or consumed. Happiness is the spiritual experience of living every minute with love, grace and gratitude.

Denis Waitley

Quote of the Day

If we are to have real peace, we must begin with the children.

Mahatma Gandhi

Food Facts

Olive oil has lots of anti-oxidants and anti-inflammatory properties to fight rheumatoid arthritis.

Mind Massage

There is a two-digit number, the second digit of which is 4 less than its first digit. Also, the number is divisible by the sum of its digits and if you do so, the quotient would be 7. Find the number.

Emotion

Condemning and damning - the tendency to be excessively critical of oneself, others, or the world.

John W. Maag

Fitness Facts

Some exercise is better than none and even small amounts of activity will have a positive effect on weight control.

Spiritual Quote

Blessed are the meek, for they shall inherit the earth.

Jesus of Nazareth

Quote of the Day

Bureaucracy defends the status quo long past the time when the quo has lost its status.

Laurence J. Peter

Food Facts

Mel Blanc (voice of Bugs Bunny) was allergic to carrots.

Mind Massage

Because cigars cannot be entirely smoked, a hobo who collects cigar butts can make a cigar to smoke out of every 3 butts that he finds. Today, he has collected 27 cigar butts. How many cigars will he be able to smoke?

Emotion

An effective way to pull yourself out of an emotional slump, like a mild depression, is to describe your emotional state out loud or in writing. When you do this exercise, try to describe yourself as if you were another person.

Fitness Facts

Exercise increases energy levels and reduces stress, which can improve your life as well as the lives of everyone else around you.

Spiritual Quote

Not a shred of evidence exists in favour of the idea that life is serious.

Brendan Gill

Quote of the Day

The true measure of a man is how he treats someone who can do him absolutely no good.

Ann Landers

Food Facts

Eggs contain most of the recognized vitamins with the exception of vitamin C.

Mind Massage

Decipher the following:

YYRUYYUBICURYY4ME

Emotion

Children who cling to parents or who don't want to leave home are stunted in their emotional, psychological growth.

Dirk Benedict

Day # 28

Fitness Facts

The length of time we live may be relatively fixed, but the quality of that time is totally within your control. By exerting some control over your well-being with exercise and moderate diet, the life you lead can become much more pleasant and healthy.

Spiritual Quote

Can one behave the same inwardly, whatever the circumstances? Can one's behaviour spring from within and not depend on what people think of you or how they look at you?

Jiddu Krishnamurti

Quote of the Day

Peace cannot be kept by force. It can only be achieved by understanding.

Albert Einstein

Food Facts

Honey is the only food that humans eat that will never go bad.

Mind Massage

Someone at a party introduces you to your mother's only sister's husband's only sister-in-law. She has no brothers.

What do you call this lady?

Emotion

Rose Wilder Lane defined freedom as self-control. Freedom is essentially a matter of achieving more and more control over one's own self.

Fitness Facts

Regular exercise among 60 and 70 year olds can improve their fitness levels to those that are normally associated with men and women that are much younger.

Spiritual Quote

We can never obtain peace in the world if we neglect the inner world and don't make peace with ourselves. World peace must develop out of inner peace. Without inner peace it is impossible to achieve world peace, external peace. Weapons themselves do not act. They have not come out of the blue. Man has made them. But even given those weapons, those terrible weapons, they cannot act by themselves. As long as they are left alone in storage they cannot do any harm. A human being must use them. Someone must push the button. Satan, the evil powers, cannot push that button. Human beings must do it.

The Dalai Lama

Quote of the Day

Many of us spend half of our time wishing for things we could have, if we didn't spend half of our time wishing.

Anonymous

Food Facts

In 1900 when Louis Lassen ground beef, broiled it, and served it between two pieces of toast, he had invented the hamburger.

Mind Massages

On one side of a card is written:

"THE SENTENCE ON THE OTHERSIDE OF THIS CARD IS TRUE."

On turning the card over you find:

"THE SENTENCE ON THE OTHERSIDE OF THIS CARD IS FALSE."

Which sentence is true?

Emotion

In the book Dictionary of Typical Command Phrases, Richard W. Wetherill states that when we are emotionally upset, we program our brains with faulty and self-destructive programming. When we are in a state of emotional upset we tend to say things such as, "If she does that again, I'll show her!" Or, "I'll never be any good at anything!" These sentences become "command phrases" which are planted in our unconscious mind where they continue to have a powerful destructive affect over us even when our emotions have calmed down.

Fitness Facts

Most people are sexual throughout their lives, with or without a partner, and some feel greater sexual freedom in their later years. On the other hand, some men and women are content to be sexually inactive.

Spiritual Quote

If you scatter thorns, don't go barefoot.

Italian Proverb

Quote of the Day

You gain strength, courage, and confidence by every experience in which you really stop to look fear in the face. You must do the thing, which you think you cannot do.

Eleanor Roosevelt

Food Facts

Chewing gum may keep you slim by boosting the metabolic rate by about 20%.

Mind Massage

How many squares are there in a 5-inch by 5-inch square grid? Note that the grid is made up of one inch by one-inch squares.

Emotion

When we identify ourselves with something — no matter what it is — we are unable to step back and view it objectively. Humans can identify themselves with just about anything, including their emotions. I should say: especially their emotions. Now, when we identify with our emotions, it is very difficult to control them; when we are immersed in our emotions, we are controlled by them. The secret of emotional control is to disengage yourself from them, to pull back, and cease identifying with your feelings and moods.

Fitness Facts

There are two indicators of age chronological age and physiological age. Chronological age is the number of years that you have lived. Physiological age reflects your biological age and tells how old your body is in respect to your health and disease status.

Spiritual Quote

The highest good is like water.
Water gives life to the ten thousand things and does not strive.
It flows in places men reject and so is like the Tao.
In dwelling, be close to the land.
In meditation, go deep in the heart.
In dealing with others, be gentle and kind.
In speech, be true.
In ruling, be just.
In business, be competent.
In action, watch the timing.

Tao Te Ching

Quote of the Day

Knowledge is proud that she knows so much; Wisdom is humble that she knows no more.

Cowper

Food Facts

Cherries are a member of the rose family.

Mind Massages

A blue house has blue bricks.

A red house has red bricks.

A yellow house has yellow bricks.

A orange house has orange bricks.

What color bricks does a green house have?

Emotion

Security represents your sense of worth, your identity, your emotional anchorage, your self-esteem, your basic personal strength or lack of it.

Stephen R. Covey

Fitness Facts

The key to a healthy, happy life style is to be patient. Rome wasn't built in a day nor will you.

Spiritual Quote

Zen mind is not Zen mind. That is, if you are attached to Zen mind, then you have a problem, and your way is very narrow. Throwing away Zen mind is correct Zen mind. Only keep the question, "What is the best way of helping other people?"

Seung Sahn

Quote of the Day

No amount of ability is of the slightest avail without honour.

Andrew Carnegie

Food Facts

Chicken is one of the few things that we eat before it's born and after it's dead.

Mind Massages

Two people enter a race in which you run to a point and back. Person A runs 20 mph to and from the point. Person B runs to the point going 10 mph and 30 mph going back.

Who came in first?

Emotion

Vivid images are like a beautiful melody that speaks to you on an emotional level. It bypasses your logic centres and even your intellect and goes to a different part of the brain.

Steven Bochco

Day # 33

Fitness Facts

It takes 3500 Calories to make a pound of fat! So, as long as you don't overeat, the calories you do eat don't have too much of a chance to turn into fat.

Spiritual Quote

Teach this triple truth to all: A generous heart, kind speech, and a life of service and compassion are the things, which renew humanity.

Buddha

Quote of the Day

To go against the dominant thinking of your friends, of most of the people you see every day, is perhaps the most difficult act of heroism you can perform.

Theodore H. White

Food Facts

Cranberries are sorted for ripeness by bouncing them; a fully ripened cranberry will bounce like a basketball.

Mind Massages

An old tea merchant in New York's Chinatown was trying to figure out how to divide 20 pounds of tea into 2-pound packets using a simple balance scale. But this merchant could only find two weights around the shop - one was 5 pounds and the other was 9 pounds.

Can you figure out how he did it?

Emotion

Learning how to monitor your automatic thoughts is not difficult. It is simply a matter of turning your attention inward and tracing back the series of thoughts which ran through your head just prior to experiencing the emotion.

Fitness Facts

If you want to keep your metabolism in high gear, add strength training to your aerobic workouts. You'll build calorie-burning muscle while you're working off excess fat.

Spiritual Quote

God doesn't look at how much we do, but with how much love we do it.

Mother Teresa

Quote of the Day

Our nation is a rainbow - red, yellow, brown, black, and white - and we're all precious in God's sight.

Jesse Jackson

Food Facts

In 1922 when Stephen Poplawski put a spinning blade at the bottom of a small electric appliance to make Horlick's malted milk shakes, he had invented the blender.

Mind Massage

Three articles - B1, B2 and B3 - were sold from a Shopping Mall. From the information given below can you discover each article's price and date on which it was sold?

The articles were sold on Nov 10, Nov 12, and Nov 14, one on each day

The article prices were $70, $75, and $80

The article B2 was not sold on Nov 10

The article sold on Nov 10 was $10 higher than that of article B3

The article sold on Nov 14 was for $75

Emotion

My emotional and intellectual response to Hiroshima was that the question of the social responsibility of a journalist was posed with greater urgency than ever.

Wilfred Burchett

Fitness Facts

If you're having trouble sleeping, you might want to try late afternoon workouts. Try not to exercise too close to bedtime, as it may make you too alert to drift off. A dip in body temperature (a cool shower) a few hours after you exercise may also help you to fall asleep.

Spiritual Quote

A man's true wealth here after is the good he does in this world to his fellow man.

Muhammad

Quote of the Day

Into the house where joy lives, happiness will gladly come.

Japanese Proverb

Food Facts

Why do people say that a poor eater "eats like a bird?" Birds eat half their own body weight in food each day!

Mind Massage

49 friends attended a campfire. After shaking hands, each of them sat on the round table and clinked their mug with the friends to his immediate left and immediate right.

How many times did the mugs clink?

Emotion

In the rush and turmoil of life, we often forget to hold onto what is good about our lives. Take a moment now, to think about all you have been given - life, freedom, others to love.

Day # 36

Fitness Facts

Every minute of your day is precious. When you train enjoy it.

Spiritual Quote

Achievement seems to be connected with action. Successful men and women keep moving. They make mistakes, but they don't quit.

Conrad Hilton

Quote of the Day

Above all things, never be afraid. The enemy who forces you to retreat is himself afraid of you at that very moment.

Andre Maurois

Food Facts

Butter and margarine are similar in calories; the difference is that butter is higher in saturated fats, while margarine generally has more unsaturated fats.

Mind Massage

Sam and Mala have a conversation.

Sam says I am certainly not over 40

Mala says I am 38 and you are at least 5 years older than me

Now Sam says you are at least 39

All the statements by the two are false. How old are they really?

Emotion

If you don't like the way you are feeling or acting, simply make changes in the way you think. This is called "cognitive therapy."

Fitness Facts

If you have been sedentary the key is to get in shape gradually. A tough workout will make you feel fatigued, sore, and stiff and may even increase the risk of a sudden heart attack.

Spiritual Quote

Every person, all the events of your life, are there because you have drawn them there. What you choose to do with them is up to you.

Richard Bach

Quote of the Day

In the province of the mind, what one believes to be true either is true or becomes true.

John Lilly

Food Facts

Casein, the main protein found in milk is the best-known neutralizer for Capsaicin, which makes hot peppers "hot" to the human mouth.

Mind Massage

What is put on a table, cut, but never eaten?

Emotion

The emotional, sexual, and psychological stereotyping of females begins when the doctor says: It's a girl.

Shirley Chisholm

Fitness Facts

It takes about 12 weeks to see measurable changes in your body once you have started an exercise program. However, you will likely notice an increase in your strength and endurance after a few weeks.

Spiritual Quote

Let your courage mount with difficulties. There would be no will if there were no resistance.

N. Sri Ram

Quote of the Day

Be as careful of the books you read, as of the company you keep; for your habits and character will be as much influenced by the former as by the latter.

Paxton Hood

Food Facts

Celery requires more calories to eat and digest than it contains.

Mind Massage

What goes up the chimney down, but can't go down the chimney up?

Emotion

Pessimism is essentially a bad habit or bad programming that was developed from being exposed to poor examples from parents, teachers, or others who provided major influences during the formative years of our lives.

Fitness Facts

Sweat is not an indicator of weight loss. The water you lose you will gain back when you drink after your workout.

Spiritual Quote

True understanding is possible only when we are fully conscious of our thought, not as an operative observer on this thought, but completely and without the intervention of a choice.

Jiddu Krishnamurti

Quote of the Day

The real voyage of discovery consists not in seeking new landscapes but in having new eyes.

Marcel Proust

Food Facts

Avocado has the highest protein and oil content of all fruits. The oil, however, is of the healthier unsaturated type.

Mind Massage

There are 4 mugs placed upturned on the table. Each mug has the same number of marbles and a statement about the number of marbles in it. The statements are: Two or Three, One or Four, Three or One, One or Two. Only one of the statements is correct. How many marbles are there under each mug?

Emotion

A man's moral worth is not measured by what his religious beliefs are but rather by what emotional impulses he has received from Nature during his lifetime.

Albert Einstein

Fitness Facts

Women with heart disease or arthritis actually experience improved daily function from involvement in various modes of physical activity.

Spiritual Quote

Loneliness and the feeling of being unwanted is the most terrible poverty.

Mother Teresa

Quote of the Day

Creativity can solve almost any problem. The creative act, the defeat of habit by originality, overcomes everything.

George Lois

Food Facts

It has been a tradition to serve fish with a slice of lemon since the Middle Ages, when people believed that lemon juice would dissolve any bones accidentally swallowed.

Mind Massage

It happens once in a minute, twice in a week, and once in a year? What is it?

Emotion

That deep emotional conviction of the presence of a superior reasoning power, which is revealed in the incomprehensible universe, forms my idea of God.

Albert Einstein

Fitness Facts

The saying "No pain, no gain." is not true. Exercise doesn't need to hurt. Muscle soreness when you do something new isn't unusual, but soreness isn't the same as pain.

Spiritual Quote

Our primary purpose in this life is to help others. If you can't help, then at least don't hurt.

The Dalai Lama

Quote of the Day

Ever tried? Ever failed? No Matter, try again, fail again, Fail better.

Samuel Beckett

Food Facts

It takes about 10 pounds of milk to make one pound of cheese.

Mind Massage

A boy found that he had a 48-inch strip of paper. He could cut an inch off every second. How long would it take for him to cut 48 pieces? He cannot fold the strip and also cannot stack two or more strips and cut them together.

Emotion

To be a human being means to possess a feeling of inferiority which constantly presses towards its own conquest. The greater the feeling of inferiority that has been experienced, the more powerful is the urge for conquest and the more violent the emotional agitation.

Alfred Adler

Fitness Facts

Studies have suggested that walking at a brisk pace for three or more hours a week can reduce your risk for coronary heart disease by 65 percent.

Spiritual Quote

The love of one's country is a splendid thing. But why should love stop at the border?

Pablo Casals

Quote of the Day

Comedy is nothing more than tragedy deferred.

Pico Iyer

Food Facts

Bakers used to be fined if their loaves were under weight, so they used to add an extra loaf to every dozen, in case they were under weight - hence, the expression "baker's dozen."

Mind Massage

Jack and Jill are playing cards for a stake of $1 a game. At the end of the evening, Jack has won 3 games and Jill has won $3. How many games did they play?

Emotion

An important aspect of emotional control is the ability to handle emotional contagion. We can become "infected" by the emotions and moods of others. You can catch both negative and positive emotions alike, such as euphoria, elation, sadness, depression, anger, grief, etc. It is important to develop some steps for protecting yourself from the negative emotions of others. Pay attention to how you feel around different people. Become aware of and label your emotional responses. Examine your emotional responses. Recognizing that a negative emotion actually belongs to someone else, may not be enough to prevent the mood from spreading to you. Never allow yourself to become contaminated with other people's negativity.

Fitness Facts

Walking at a brisk pace (at 15-minute or 4 mph mile) burns nearly as many calories as jogging over the same distance. Jogging takes less time to cover the same distance and benefits the bones; however, it may be too strenuous for some. Train don't strain.

Spiritual Quotes

The cave you fear to enter holds the treasure you seek.

Joseph Campbell

Quote of the Day

The wisest men follow their own direction.

Euripides

Food Facts

When a source of Vitamin C (orange, lemon, grapefruit, strawberry, tomato, potato, etc.) is eaten with meat or cooked dry beans, the body makes better use of the iron in the protein food.

Mind Massage

Bill is at a family reunion. Uncle John tells Bill that Bill has one long lost sister, who always speaks the truth. He points at a table, where three women are sitting and says, "One of those ladies is your long lost sister. Go meet her." Bill goes over to the table as told. "I am your long lost sister," says Sharon. "She's lying, I am your long lost sister," says Barbara with a smirk. Julia looks at Bill and says, "Two of us always lie."

Which one is Bill's long lost sister?

Emotion

Painful as it may be, a significant emotional event can be the catalyst for choosing a direction that serves us - and those around us - more effectively. Look for the learning.

Louisa May Alcott

Fitness Facts

For complete fitness you need to include aerobic exercise, strength training, and stretching.

Spiritual Quote

Life is both pleasure and pain, is it not? ... But why should we cling to pleasure and avoid pain? Why not merely live with both? ... If you cling to pleasure what happens? You get attached, do you not?

Jiddu Krishnamurti

Quote of the Day

I used to dread getting older because I thought I would not be able to do all the things I wanted to do, but now that I am older I find that I don't want to do them.

Nancy Astor

Food Facts

The dish Chop-Suey was created by Chinese immigrants in California.

Mind Massage

A farmer built a fence around his 25 cows in a square region. He built it in such a way that one could see 5 poles from any of the four sides. What is the minimum number of poles the farmer must have used?

Emotion

Emotional occasions, especially violent ones, are extremely potent in precipitating mental rearrangements. The sudden and explosive ways in which love, jealousy, guilt, fear, remorse, or anger can seize upon one are known to everybody.... And emotions that come in this explosive way seldom leave things as they found them.

William James

Fitness Facts

If you aren't already Mr. Universe or Ms. America chances are you won't be now, so set reasonable fitness goals so that they can be reasonably attained.

Spiritual Quote

A student asked Soen Nakagawa during a meditation retreat, "I am very discouraged. What should I do?" Soen replied, "Encourage others."

Soen Nakagawa

Quote of the Day

Work is not always required... there is such a thing as sacred idleness, the cultivation of which is now fearfully neglected.

George McDonald

Food Facts

The longer that fruits or vegetables sit around, the more nutrients they lose. But fruits and vegetables grown for freezing are usually frozen right away and, therefore, have less time to lose their nutrients.

Mind Massage

An anthropologist discovers an isolated tribe whose written alphabet contains only six letters (call the letters A, B, C, D, E and F). The tribe has a taboo against using the same letter twice in the same word. It's never done.

If each different sequence of letters constitutes a different word in the language, what is the maximum number of six-letter words that the language can employ?

Emotion

In The Path of Least Resistance, Robert Fritz states that most people believe circumstances are the driving force of their lives. In other words, he states that people believe that they are forced to either respond to or react against their circumstances and that they tend not to believe that they can make choices independent of their circumstances.

Fitness Facts

Exercise may make you feel tired at first, but the tiredness won't last long.

Spiritual Quote

Whatever you have in your mind - forget it; whatever you have in your hand - give it; whatever is to be your fate - face it!

Abu Sa'id

Quote of the Day

You always pass failure on the way to success.

Mickey Rooney

Food Facts

Half of the world's population live on a staple diet of rice.

Mind Massage

If you were to dial any 7 digits on a telephone in random order, what is the probability that you will dial your own phone number?

Assume that your telephone number is 7-digits.

Emotion

The worst drugs are as bad as anybody's told you. It's just a dumb trip, which I can't condemn people if they get into it, because one gets into it for one's own personal, social, emotional reasons. It's something to be avoided if one can help it.

John Lennon

Day # 47

Fitness Facts

When you exercise wear clothing that is comfortable and allows you to move freely. Also make sure your clothes are cool enough for when your body begins to heat up.

Spiritual Quote

The secret of attraction is to love yourself. Attractive people judge neither themselves nor others. They are open to gestures of love. They think about love, and express their love in every action. They know that love is not a mere sentiment, but the ultimate truth at the heart of the universe.

Deepak Chopra

Quote of the Day

If you really do put a small value on upon yourself, rest assured that the rest of the world will not raise your price.

Anonymous

Food Facts

A low calorie diet won't help you loose weight. Low calorie diets may appear at first to help, but soon all weight loss comes to a halt when your metabolism shuts down. The key is to eat 6 "small" meals a day and keep the fat burning engines at full speed. Don't starve yourself.

Mind Massage

I have four wings, but cannot fly
I never laugh and never cry
on the same spot I'm always found,
toiling away with little sound.
What am I?

Emotion

Start by remembering what is important. Most of what stresses us are the things that don't matter in the long run. Being cut off in traffic, breaking a fingernail, not being able to buy the newest gadget, someone else's rudeness—these are not worth worrying about. What really matters is whether we are fair and caring.

Fitness Facts

Proper footwear should be comfortable by providing adequate arch support and sole protection.

Spiritual Quote

If you don't get what you want, you suffer; if you get what you don't want, you suffer; even when you get exactly what you want, you still suffer because you can't hold on to it forever. Your mind is your predicament. It wants to be free of change. Free of pain, free of the obligations of life and death. But change is a law, and no amount of pretending will alter that reality.

Dan Millman

Quote of the Day

Focus + Determination + Hard Work = Talent

Frank Moffatt

Food Facts

The only vegetable or fruit which is never sold frozen, canned, processed or cooked is lettuce. Lettuce is only sold fresh.

Mind Massage

As I was traveling to Calgary I saw a man with 7 wives, with 7 kittens, in 7 sacks, and with 7 drinks on a bike.

How many people/things are going to Calgary?

Emotion

In order to experience emotion we need to first interpret an event or stimulus and assign meaning to it. Although we may not have control over the event, we can learn how to control our interpretation process, thus increasing our emotional control.

Fitness Facts

Today there are many options when one decides, where, when and with whom to workout. Remember, the choice is yours if you aren't happy, change it.

Spiritual Quote

You yourself, as much as anybody in the entire universe, deserve your love and affection.

Buddha

Quote of the Day

A non-doer is very often a critic - that is, someone who sits back and watches doers, and then waxes philosophically about how the doers are doing. It's easy to be a critic, but being a doer requires effort, risk, and change.

Dr. Wayne Dyer

Food Facts

Shredded wheat was the first breakfast cereal to ever be produced.

Mind Massage

Which candle burns longer a blue candle or a green candle?

Emotion

The quality of your life is dependent upon the quality of the life of your cells. If the bloodstream is filled with waste products, the resulting environment does not promote a strong, vibrant, healthy cell life - nor a biochemistry capable of creating a balanced emotional life for an individual.

Anthony Robbins

Fitness Fact

An exercise program can be a fun addition to your week that doesn't have to cramp your schedule. Do a variety of exercises, set realistic goals, and enjoy yourself.

Spiritual Quote

The great awareness comes slowly, piece by piece. The path of spiritual growth is a path of lifelong learning. The experience of spiritual power is basically a joyful one.

Scott Peck

Quote of the Day

Don't be pushed by your problems. Be led by your dreams.

Anonymous

Food Facts

Refried beans aren't really what they seem. Although their name seems like a reasonable translation of Spanish frijoles refritos, the fact is the beans aren't fried twice. In Spanish, refritos literally means "well-fried" not "re-fried."

Mind Massage

Only one color, but not one size
Stuck at the bottom, but easily flies
Present in the sun, but not in the rain
Doing no harm, and feeling no pain

What am I?

Emotional

Scientific knowledge and the wisdom of the ages agree the healthiest people live lives based on trying to make the world a better place for all living creatures. You cannot be emotionally fit if your heart is full of anger or hate.

Fifty Fitness Exercises

Cardio Exercises

There are many variations of cardio exercises. We have listed 4 here but please feel free to do what ever works best for you. There are no descriptions for these exercises as they are self explanatory.

1) **Tread Mill** (Walking or Jogging)
2) **Elliptical**
3) **Exercise Bike**
4) **Stairmaster or Stair Climber**

Neck Exercises

5) **Manual Neck Resistance** - Place the heel of your hand on your forehead. Apply pressure with your hand. Resist against this pressure with your neck muscles. Press as hard as you can, but don't over do it and run the risk of an injury.
6) **Neck Stretch** - Turn your head as far as you can so your chin is over, or close to over, your shoulder, and then hold for 20 seconds. Repeat the stretch on the other side. Don't hold your breath.

Shoulder Exercises

7) **Military Press** – Sitting on a bench, grab the barbell with a wider than shoulder width grip. Push the barbell directly upward until it is at arms length above your shoulders. Lower the barbell back to starting position. Repeat for 8 to 12 repetitions.

8) **Seated Dumbbell Press** - Sit on an upright bench. Lift two dumbbells to your shoulders. Your palms should be facing forwards. Push the dumbbells directly upward until your arms are straight but not locked out. Lower the dumbbells back to the starting position at the top of your chest. Repeat for 8 to 12 repetitions.

9) **Side Lateral Raises** - Stand with your feet shoulder width apart. Hold the dumbbells in front of your body with your palms facing each other. Keep your elbows bent at approximately 90-degrees. Raise the dumbbells out to the sides and upwards to shoulder level. Hold this position for a second to maximize the contraction. Lower the dumbbells back to the starting position. Repeat for 8 to 12 repetitions.

10) **Front Lateral Raises** - Stand with your feet shoulder width apart. Hold the dumbbells in front of your body with your palms facing in towards your legs. Slightly bend your elbows. Raise the dumbbells to the front and upwards to shoulder level. Hold this position for a second to maximize the contraction. Lower the dumbbells back to the starting position. Repeat for 8 to 12 repetitions.

11) **Bent Lateral Raises** - Bend over at the waist with your knees slightly bent and your feet shoulder width apart. Hold the dumbbells at arms length in front of you with your palms facing each other and

your elbows slightly bent. Raise the dumbbells to the back and upwards as far as possible. Hold this position for a second to maximize the contraction. Lower the dumbbells back to the starting position. Repeat for 8 to 12 repetitions.

12) **Barbell Shrugs** - Bend your legs and lift the barbell until it is at arms length in front of you. Keep your knees slightly bent to take the stress off of your lower back. Without moving your arms, lift the barbell upwards with your shoulders as high as you can. Hold this position for a second at the top of the movement to maximize the contraction. Lower the barbell back to the starting position. Repeat for 8 to 12 repetitions.

13) **Shoulder Stretch** - This stretch will mainly affect the front of the shoulder (the deltoid muscle). Place one arm across the front of your body. With the opposite hand, grasp your elbow. Now, pull your arm across your body without twisting your torso.

Arm Exercises (Biceps)

14) **Standing Barbell Curls** – Hold the barbell with an underhand grip. Stand with your feet shoulder width apart. Let the barbell hang in front of you at arms length. Keep your elbows close to your side at all times. Use your biceps to curl the barbell up to shoulder level. Hold the weight in the top position for a second to maximize the contraction of your biceps. Now slowly lower the barbell to the starting position. Repeat for 8 to 12 repetitions.

15) **Standing Dumbbell Curls** - Hold the dumbbells with an underhand grip. Stand with your feet

shoulder width apart. Let the dumbbells hang at arms length on each side of your body. Keep your elbows close to your sides at all times. Use your biceps to curl the dumbbells up to shoulder level. Hold the weight in the top position for a second to maximize the contraction of your biceps. Now slowly lower the dumbbells to the starting position. Repeat for 8 to 12 repetitions.

16) **Dumbbell Concentration Curls** - Sit legs apart at the end of an exercise bench. Brace your elbow against the inside of your knee and fully straighten your arm. Use your bicep to curl the dumbbell up to shoulder level. Hold the weight in the top position for a second or two to maximize the contraction of your biceps. Now slowly lower the dumbbell to the starting position. Repeat for 8 to 12 repetitions. Do the same for each arm.

17) **Bicep-Wall Stretch** - Place the palm, inner elbow, and shoulder of one arm against the wall. Keeping the arm in contact with the wall, exhale and slowly turn your body around, to feel the stretch in your biceps and chest.

Arm Exercises (Triceps)

18) **Lying Barbell Extensions** - Lie on your back on a flat bench. Your feet should be shoulder width apart on each side of the bench. It is best to have a training partner hand you the barbell. Hold the bar narrower than shoulder width. Press the barbell up until it is at arms length above your shoulders. Lower the barbell to within an inch or so above your forehead. Using your triceps push the bar back up to the starting position. Repeat for 8 to 12 repetitions.

19) **Tricep Dumbbell Extensions** - Stand with your feet shoulder width apart. Lift the dumbbell so that it is straight above your shoulder. Slightly bend your knees to take the pressure off of your lower back. Slowly lower the dumbbell to a position behind your head and where your elbow is at a 90-degree angle. Slowly lift the dumbbell back to the starting position. Repeat for 8 to 12 repetitions. Do the same for each arm.

20) **Tricep Pushdowns** - Attach a short bar or rope apparatus to an overhead pulley. Stand with your feet shoulder width apart. Grab the bar or rope with an overhand grip. Hold your arms at a 90-degree to your body and keep your elbows against your sides at all times during the exercise. Push the bar down until your arms are straight. Hold this position for a second to maximize the contraction. Slowly lower the weight until the arms are again at 90-degrees. Repeat for 8 to 12 repetitions.

21) **Tricep Dumbbell Kick Backs** - Stand beside a flat exercise bench. Bend over until your upper body is parallel to the floor. Place one hand on the bench to support yourself. Hold the weight at a 90-degree angle to your upper body. Lift the dumbbell until your arm is straight. Hold this position for a second or two to maximize the contraction in the triceps. Slowly return the dumbbell to the starting position. Repeat for 8 to 12 repetitions.

22) **Tricep Stretch** - Hold one end of a towel in your right hand. Raise and bend your right arm to drape the towel down your back. Keep your right arm in this position and continue holding onto the towel. Reach behind your lower back and grasp the bottom end of the towel with your left hand. Climb your left hand progressively higher up the

towel, which also pulls your right arm down. Continue until your hands touch, or as close as you can comfortably go. Change arms.

Forearm Exercise

23) **Reverse Curls** – Hold a barbell palms down and shoulder width apart. Stand with your feet shoulder width apart. Let the barbell hang in front of you. Keep your elbows close to your sides at all times. Curl the barbell up to shoulder level. Hold this position for a second to maximize the contraction. Slowly lower the barbell to the starting position. Repeat for 8 to 12 repetitions.

Wrist Exercises

24) **Wrist Curl Rolls** – At one end of a 6 or 7 foot piece of rope tie a 5 or 10 lb weight. At the other end of the rope tie a dumbbell bar or twelve inch piece of wood dowel. Hold the end with the dumbbell bar at shoulder height, arms extended, palms down. Begin rolling up the rope by first twisting your right wrist forward and then by twisting your left wrist forward. Continue until you have rolled the weight up to the bar. Now reverse the action until the weight has been rolled back down to ground level. Repeat 4 times or as many times as possible.

25) **Dumbbell Wrist Curls** - Keep the palms of your hands facing up. Sit on a flat exercise bench with your forearms resting on your thighs and your wrists hanging over the ends of your knees. Curl the dumbbells up using only your wrists. Hold the dumbbells at the top position for a second to maximize the contraction. Slowly lower the

dumbbells back to the starting position. Repeat for 8 to 12 repetitions.

26) **Wrist Stretch** - Place hands together, in praying position. Slowly raise elbows so arms are parallel to ground, keeping hands flat against each other. Hold position for 10 to 30 seconds.

Chest Exercises

27) **Flat Barbell Bench Press** - Lie down on the flat bench press. Place your feet flat on the floor or on the end of the bench. Hold the bar with a wider than shoulder width grip. Once you have lifted the bar from the rack, position the bar over your chest. Lower the barbell until your elbows are at 90-degrees to the floor, parallel with the bench. Then press the bar back up to a position just short of locking out your elbows. Repeat for 8 to 12 repetitions. Lowering the bar past 90-degrees may cause serious shoulder injury.

28) **Incline Dumbbell Press** - Lower the dumbbells until your elbows are at a 90-degree angle to your shoulders. Then press the dumbbells back up to a position just short of locking out your elbows. Repeat for 8 to 12 repetitions. This exercise would require an incline weight lifting bench to be performed at home. Lowering the dumbbells past 90-degrees may cause serious shoulder injury.

29) **Decline Barbell Bench Press** - Lower the barbell until your elbows are at a 90-degree angle to your shoulders. Then press the bar back up to a position just short of locking out your elbows. Repeat for 8 to 12 repetitions. This exercise would require a decline weight lifting bench to be performed

at home. Lowering the bar past 90-degrees may cause serious shoulder injury.

30) **Dumbbell Bench Press** - Lie down on a flat bench. Lower the dumbbells until your elbows are at a 90-degree angle to the floor, parallel with the bench. Then press the dumbbells back up to a position just short of locking out your elbows. Repeat for 8 to 12 repetitions. Lowering the dumbbells past 90-degrees may cause serious shoulder injury.

31) **Push Ups** - Lie face down on the floor with your palms on the ground beside your body. Keeping your legs and torso straight, push yourself up with your arms until they are extended. Lower yourself slowly until your chest nearly touches the floor. Hold this position for a second. Again push yourself back up to where you started. Repeat for 8 to 12 repetitions.

32) **Corner Stretch for Chest** - Forget all your grade school fears - standing in a corner is one of the best stretching exercises. Stand facing a corner with one hand on each wall, about chin level. Lean forward until you feel a stretch in your chest and shoulders. Repeat this muscle stretching technique for flexibility.

Back Exercises

33) **One Arm Dumbbell Row** – Put one knee on a flat exercise bench and one foot on the floor. For support place one hand on the bench. Hold the dumbbell with your other hand. Keep your back level with the floor. Keeping your elbow close to your side, slowly pull the dumbbell directly upwards until it touches your side. Hold it there for a second to maximize the contraction. Lower

the dumbbell slowly, back to the starting position. Repeat for 8 to 12 repetitions. Do the same for both arms.

34) **Bent Over Barbell Row** - Bend over and grab a barbell with your hands shoulder width apart. Keep your knees slightly bent. Lift the bar keeping your arms straight. Keep your upper body at a 45-degree angle to the floor. Using just your arms raise the barbell to your stomach. Hold this position for a second to maximize the contraction. Lower the bar until your arms are straight, but don't let the barbell touch the floor.

    Repeat for 8 to 12 repetitions.

35) **Lat Pulldowns** – Hold the bar with your hands slightly wider than shoulder width apart. Pull the bar down in front of your head until the bar nearly touches the top of your chest. Hold this position for a second to maximize the contraction. Slowly straighten your arms back to the starting position. Repeat for 8 to 12 repetitions.

36) **Back Extension Using The Stability Ball** - Lie face down on a stability ball. Position yourself so you are balanced directly over the ball with your toes or the sides of your feet on he floor. Lower your upper body towards the ground. Place your hands on your chest and raise your upper body as high as possible. Repeat for 8 to 12 repetitions.

37) **Back Stretch** - With this exercise, you release all that tension and stress you're holding in your shoulders and upper back. Kneel with your knees under hips and hands under shoulders. Spread the fingers out on the floor with palms flat and contract the abdominal muscles to bring the head, neck, and back in alignment. Inhale and tip the

hip bones towards the ceiling while drawing the shoulders back and down away from your ears and look up. Exhale and tuck the chin while pulling your belly towards your spine. Round the back and feel a stretch down your spine. Repeat for 4 to 6 breaths, moving smoothly between each move.

Abdominal Exercises

38) **Bicycle Manoeuvre** - Lie flat on the floor with your lower back against the ground. Put your hands beside your head. Bring your knees up to about a 45-degree angle and slowly go through a bicycle pedal motion. Touch your left elbow to your right knee and then your right elbow to your left knee.

39) **Crunch on an Exercise Ball** - Sit on the exercise ball with your feet flat on the floor. Let the ball roll back slowly and lie back until your thighs and torso are parallel with the floor. Contract your abdominals raising your torso to no more than 45 degrees.

Leg Exercises

40) **Leg Press** – Place your feet shoulder width apart on the platform. Grasp the handles beside the seat. Push back against the platform. Don't completely straighten the leg to avoid injury. Return to starting position. Repeat for 8 to 12 repetitions.

41) **Box Squats** – Standing shoulder width apart, hold the bar wider than shoulder width apart. Position the bar across the top of your shoulders and not on your neck. Lift the bar off of the rack with your legs. Look forward. Bend your legs and squat

down. Your knees should be directly over your toes as you do the movement. At the bottom of this squat, sit back on the box and pause for a second before coming up. Repeat for 8 to 12 repetitions.

42) **Lunges** - Step out a couple feet with one leg, keep your toes pointed forward and your front foot flat on the floor. Bend your front leg until your knee is at a 90-degree angle to the floor, and your back leg should also bend until it is at a 90-degree angle. Push up and return to the starting position. Repeat for 8 to 12 repetitions, and then do the same with the other leg out front. You can also do lunges with your back leg on a bench; this will give you a better range of motion.

43) **Leg Extensions** – Place your feet beneath the roller pads and hold the handles at the sides of the machine. Straighten your legs, lifting the weight. Pause at the top for a second or two to enhance the contraction. Lower your legs slowly to the starting position. Repeat for 8 to 12 repetitions.

44) **Lying Leg Curls** - Hook your feet beneath the roller pads and hold the handles at the sides of the machine. Curl your legs, lifting the weight. Pause at the top for a second or two to enhance the contraction. Lower your legs slowly to the starting position. Repeat for 8 to 12 repetitions.

45) **Quad Stretch** - For lean sexy legs, do the standing quadriceps stretch. Pull your foot up, with the knee bent and the thigh straight up and down, next to the supporting leg. During this muscle stretching, don´t pull the leg back and to the side, which stresses the knee, and don´t lean forward, which reduces range of motion and decreases stretching effectiveness.

46) **Hamstring Stretch** - For a good hamstring stretch, lie on your back on the floor. Leave one leg extended on the floor and raise the other, knee straight, until you feel the stretch in your hamstring. Loop a towel around your leg and hold the ends in your hands to make it easier.

Calve Exercises

47) **Standing Calve Raise** - Place your head between the shoulder pads on the calf machine. With your feet shoulder width apart, place the balls of your feet on the foot block, toes pointing forward. Keep your legs straight during the entire movement. Slowly lower your heels until your calve muscles stretch down as far as possible. Hold the stretched position for a second and then rise up as high as you can on your toes. Hold this position for a second to enhance the contraction in the calves. Repeat for 8 to 12 repetitions. This exercise would require a standing calve machine to be performed at home.

48) **Seated Calve Raise** - Adjust the kneepads so they are snug and comfortable. With your feet shoulder width apart place the balls of your feet on the foot block, toes pointing forward. Raise your heals up as high as you can. Hold this position for a second to enhance the contraction in the calves. Lower your heels until your calve muscles stretch as far as possible. Hold the stretched position for a second. Repeat for 8 to 12 repetitions. This exercise would require a Standing calve machine to be performed at home.

49) **One Leg Calve Raise** - Standing on one leg, place the ball of your foot on a block with your heels

hanging over the edge. Hold onto something for balance. Keep your knee straight. Slowly lower your heel until your calf muscle stretches as far as possible. Hold the stretched position for a second and then rise up as high as you can on your toes. Hold this position for a second to enhance the contraction of the calf. Repeat for 8 to 12 repetitions. Repeat with the other leg.

50) **Calf Stretch** - Give those calves the muscle stretching of their life! You should stretch your calves two ways with two different stretching exercises. First is the usual way where you lean against a wall, step back with the leg to be stretched, knee straight, then keep your heel down and push your hips forward until you feel the stretching in your calf. Second, keep the same position but bend your knee, which will give a better stretch to the soleus muscle and the achilles´ tendon.

Methodical Mind Massages ~ *Answers 1 to 50*

Answer Q # 1

- A stocking or a sock
- Usually, it is filled with your foot in the morning and taken off (i.e. emptied) at night. But on Christmas, it is emptied at night so that Santa can fill it with gifts. Then it is emptied in the morning by children.

Answer Q # 2

He was Walking. He is a Bus driver. But it does not say that he was driving.

Answer Q # 3

- The next two letters are N and T.
- The pattern is - the last letter of the words onE, twO, threE, fouR, etc...
- Hence, the next two letters are seveN and eighT.

Answer Q # 4

For the sake of explanation, let's identify a 4 gallon bucket as Bucket P and a 9 gallon bucket as Bucket Q.

- Fill bucket Q with 9 gallons of water
- Pour 4 gallons water from bucket Q to bucket P
- Empty bucket P
- Pour 4 gallons water from bucket Q to bucket P
- Empty bucket P
- Pour 1 gallon water from bucket Q to bucket P
- Fill bucket Q with 9 gallons of water
- Pour 3 gallons water from bucket Q to bucket P
- 9 gallon bucket now contains 6 gallons of water

Answer Q # 5

- Doc, Happy, Smelly, Sneezy, Stumpy, Sleepy, Grumpy, Dopey, Droopy, Bashful

Answer Q # 6

- Repeat after me.

Answer Q # 7

- There are total 2 couples and so: the grandfather and grandmother, their son and his wife, and their son. So 5 people in total.
- Three - grandfather & grandmother + son & wife + son.

Answer Q # 8

- There are 11 letters in "The Alphabet."

Answer Q # 9

- Darkness, Fog, Smoke.

Answer Q # 10

- The sign-maker will need 192 zeroes.
- Divide 1000 building numbers into groups of 100 each as follow:

  (1...100), (101...200), (201...300) ... (901...1000)
- For the first group, the sign-maker will need 11 zeroes.
- For group numbers 2 to 9, he will require 20 zeroes each.
- And for group number 10, he will require 21 zeroes.
- The total numbers of zeroes required are = 11 + 8*20 + 21 = 11 + 160 + 21 = 192

Answer Q # 11

- It is given that - (sack of potatoes) + (box of mangoes) = (barrel of pickles) + (crate of cherries) and 2 * (crate of cherries) = (box of mangoes)
- Add both the equations
- (sack of potatoes) + (box of mangoes) + 2 * (crate of cherries) = (barrel of pickles) + (crate of cherries) + (box of mangoes)
- (sack of potatoes) + (crate of cherries) = (barrel of pickles)
- (sack of potatoes) + (crate of cherries) = 60 kgs

Answer Q # 12

- It is a one floor house, and a one floor house does

not have stairs. Hence, there is no question of colour of stairs as there are no stairs.

Answer Q # 13

- ALL the children are girls, so half are girls and so is the other half.

Answer Q # 14

- There are total 12 members in Mr. Smith's family. Mr. Smith and his wife Debi, nine sons and one daughter.
- Mr. Smith does not have 9 daughters. There is only one daughter and she is the only sister. If there are 9 daughters, then each son will have 9 sisters and not just a one.

Answer Q # 15

- Let distance between home and church be D.
- A person took 4 hours to reach church. So speed while traveling towards church is D/4.
- Similarly, he took 3 hours to reach home. So speed while coming back is D/3.
- There is a speed difference of 7*D/12, which is because the wind is helping the person in one direction and slowing him in the other direction. Average the 2 speeds, and you have the speed that person can travel in no wind, which is 7*D/24.
- Hence, person will take D / (7*D/24) hours to travel distance D which is 24/7 hours.
- Answer is 3 hours 25 minutes 42 seconds

Answer Q # 16

- One of them was a 10 cent coin and the other one was a 50 cent piece.
- The boy got two coins: a 50 cent piece and a 10 cent coin. One of them was not a 50 cent piece. But the other one was.

Answer Q # 17

- It's simple.
- Let's find the possible places horses can finish. Possibilities are:
- Whisper - 2,3,4 (not 5th as Eclipse came one place after him)
- Lightning - 2,3,4
- Eclipse - 3,4,5
- Thunder - 1,3 (not 4th & 5th as Sunshine is two place after him)
- Sunshine - 3,5
- So the result is: 1 Thunder, 2 Lightning, 3 Sunshine, 4 Whisper, 5 Eclipse

Answer Q # 18

- It doesn't matter how you put the marbles in the jar.
- Chances of picking a Red marble are the same. i.e. 50%

Answer Q # 19

- The tape was rewound, which is not possible if it was a suicide.
- The cops knew this was a murder because if it

was suicide, the man would be dead and unable to rewind the tape and get it ready for the cops to just push the play button and hear the story.

Answer Q # 20

- The next row is 1113213211
- Starting with the second line, every line describes the line before it. In writing, it is:

  One One

  Two Ones

  One Two One One

  etc.

Answer Q # 21

- There are 7 members in Mr. Powell's family. Mother & Father of Mr. Powell, Mr. & Mrs. Powell, his son and two daughters.
- Family Tree - Mother & Father of Mr. Powell + Mr. & Mrs. Powell + one son & two Daughters

Answer Q # 22

- The soldier said, "You will put me to the sword." *The soldier has to say a Paradox to save himself. If his statement is true, he will be hanged, which is not the sword and hence false. If his statement is false, he will be put to the sword, which will make it true. A Paradox !!!

Answer Q # 23

- A sieve

Answer Q # 24

- He is a Preacher (Priest) or a Judge, who has the authority to legally marry people.

Answer Q # 25

- Let's assume that the first digit is N. Hence, the second digit is (N-4) and the number is = 10N + (N-4) = 11N - 4
- Now, it is given that the number is divisible by the sum of its digit and the quotient would be 7.
- (11N - 4) / (N + N - 4) = 7
- (11N - 4) / (2N - 4) = 7
- (11N - 4) = 7 * (2N - 4)
- 11N - 4 = 14N - 28
- 3N = 24
- N = 8
- Thus, the first digit is 8, the second digit is 4 and the required number is 84.

Answer Q # 26

- He makes 9 originals from the 27 butts he found, and after he smokes them he has 9 butts left for another 3 cigars. And then he has 3 butts for another cigar.
- So 9+3+1=13

Answer Q # 27

- Too wise are you, too wise you be. I see you are, too wise for me.

Answer Q # 28

- Mother or Mom.

Answer Q # 29

- It's a Paradox. Both the sentences are contradictory to each other. If you say that the first sentence is true, then the second will contradict it and vice versa.

Answer Q # 30

- There are 55 squares in a 5 by 5 grid.
- There are 25 squares of one grid
- There are 16 squares of four grids i.e. 2 by 2
- There are 9 squares of nine grids i.e. 3 by 3
- There are 4 squares of sixteen grids i.e. 4 by 4
- There is 1 square of twenty-five girds i.e. 5 by 5
- Hence, there are total 25 + 16 + 9 + 4 + 1 = 55 squares.
- You must have noticed that the total number squares possible of each size is always a perfect square i.e. 25, 16, 9, 4, 1

Answer Q # 31

- A green house doesn't have bricks.
- A greenhouse (also called a glasshouse or hothouse) is a building where plants are cultivated.

Answer Q # 32

- Note that initially the speed of Person A (20 mph) was twice the speed of Person B (10 mph). Hence, when Person A (20 mph forward) reached the point, Person B (10 mph forward) was halfway. When Person A (20 mph back) finished, Person B (still 10 mph forward) reached the point.

❖ Thus, Person A wins the race and by that time Person B covers only half the distance, no matter how far the point is!!!

Answer Q # 33

❖ Answer Q # 32 There are many ways to do it.

❖ Get 4 pounds of tea using 9-pound and 5-pound weights.

❖ Using the balance, divide this 4 pounds of tea into 2 equal parts of 2 pounds each.

❖ Using this 2-pound tea packet as a make-shift weight, divide the remaining tea into 9 packets of 2-pounds each.

Answer Q # 34

❖ B2 was not sold on Nov 10 (clue 3). Neither was it B3 (clue 4). It must have been B1, which was sold on Nov 10, and must have been sold for $80.

❖ Hence, B3 must have been sold for $70, and B2 must have been sold for $75.

❖ Also, B2 was sold on Nov 14. It ollows that B3 was sold on Nov 12.

❖ B1 - $80 - Nov 10, B2 - $75 - Nov 14, B3 - $70 - Nov 12

Answer Q # 35

❖ Let's assume that everyone clinked their mug with a friend to his left only. It means that there are total

49 clinks. Now the right clink of each person is left clink of the person on right which has already happened. Hence, there are only 49 clinks.

Answer Q # 36

- Let's invert the teaser and read it like this :
- Sam says I am certainly over 40
- Mala says I am not 38 and you are at most 4 years older than me
- Now Sam says you are at most 38
- From first the statement it is clear that Sam is over 40. Also, from the next 2 statements it is clear that Mala is less then 38. Hence the possibilities are:
- Sam = 41, 42, 43, 44, 45, ... and Mala = 37, 36, 35, 34, 33, ...
- It also says that the difference between their age is maximum 4 years. Hence, there is only one possible pair i.e. 41 and 37, all other combination are more then 4.
- Hence the answer - Sam is 41 and Mala is 37.

Answer Q # 37

- A deck of cards

Answer Q # 38

- An umbrella

Answer Q # 39

- As it is given that only one of the four statement is correct, the correct number can not appear in more than one statement. If it appears in more than one statement, then more than one statement will be correct.

- ❖ Hence, there are 4 marbles under each mug.

Answer Q # 40

- ❖ Letter 'e'

Answer Q # 41

- ❖ To get 48 pieces, the boy has to put only 47 cuts. i.e. he can cut 46 pieces in 46 seconds. After getting 46 pieces, he will have a 2 inch long piece. He can cut it into two with just a one cut in 1 second. Hence, total of 47 seconds.

Answer Q # 42

- ❖ They played a total of 9 games. Jack won 3 games and Jill won 6 games.
- ❖ If Jack has won three games and Jill has won $3, she lost a dollar for each loss. Therefore, she has won 6 and lost 3 to make $3, and he won the other 3 that she lost!

Answer Q # 43

- ❖ Let's assume that Sharon is Bill's long lost sister. It means that Sharon is telling the truth and Barbara is lying. If so, the statement made by Julia is contradictory. Hence, Sharon is not the sister.
- ❖ Barbara is also not the sister, by same reasoning as above.

- Let's assume that Julia is Bill's long lost sister. It means that Julia is telling the truth and other two are lying. Hence, Julia is Bill's long lost sister.

Answer Q # 44

- One pole at each corner and three poles along each side, so that one can always see 5 poles from either of the four sides. The corner pole is shared by two sides, hence reducing the number of poles to 16.

Answer Q # 45

- It is a simple permutation problem of arranging 6 letters to get different six-letter words. And it can be done in 6 ways i.e. 720 ways.
- In other words, the first letter can be any of the given 6 letters (A through F). Then, whatever the first letter is, the second letter will always be from the remaining 5 letters (as same letter cannot be used twice), and the third letter will always be from the remaining 4 letters, and so on. Thus, the different possible six-letter words are 6*5*4*3*2*1 = 720

Answer Q # 46

- There are 10 digits i.e. 0-9. The first digit can be dialed in 10 ways. The second digit can be dialed in 10 ways. The third digit can be dialed in 10 ways. And so on.....
- Thus,7-digitcanbedialedin10*10*10*10*10*10*10 = (10,000,000) ways. And, you have just one telephone number. Hence, the possibility that you will dial your own number is 1 in 10,000,000.

- Note that 0123456 may not be a valid 7-digit telephone number. But while dialing in random order, that is one of the possible 7-digit numbers which you may dial.

Answer Q # 47

- A windmill. It has four wings but cannot fly. It never laughs or cries. It is always found on the same spot. And it produces little sound whenever little wind is there.

Answer Q # 48

- One man is traveling to Calgary. It said, "I saw a man with 7 wives, with 7 kittens, in 7 sacks, and with 7 drinks, on a bike." He only saw them, so they did not count. Hence, he is the only person that is actually going.

Answer Q # 49

- Neither, they both burn shorter. This is a tricky riddle as candles don't burn longer, they burn shorter. Also, the color of the candles is just to misguide you.

Answer Q # 50

- A shadow is always Black and comes in different sizes. It is always stuck at the bottom (i.e. ground) but easily flies. It's always present in the sun, but not in the rain. And it is doing no harm and feeling no pain.

Appendix

Please feel free to make up your own program – try to work each body part at least once a week. There is no perfect plan. The only plan that won't work is the one that you don't use. Again, if you are unsure of your current health condition please visit a doctor first prior to starting a workout program.

Routine # 1

Rotate Chest & Shoulders with Arms & Back with Legs and Abs – change exercises daily

Monday

CHEST - Incline Dumbbell Presses
1 set x 15 reps
2-3 sets x 10 reps

SHOULDER TRAINING – Military Press
3-4 x 12-15

Wednesday

BICEPS - Standing Barbell Curls
3 x 15

TRICEPS - Lying Overhead Triceps Extensions
4-6 x 15

FOREARM & WRIST – Reverse curls
3 x 15

BACK MUSCLES - One-Arm Dumbbell Rows
3 sets x 12-15 reps

Friday

LEG MUSCLES - Leg Presses
4-8 x 8-15

Lying Leg Curls
3-6 x 8-10

Seated Calf Raises
3-4 x 12

AB EXERCISES - Crunches
4 x 25

Routine # 2

Rotate Chest, Back, Abs & Shoulders with Arms & Legs – change exercises daily

Monday

CHEST - Incline Dumbbell Presses
1 set x 15 reps
2-3 sets x 10 reps

BACK MUSCLES - One-Arm Dumbbell Rows
3 sets x 12-15 reps

SHOULDER TRAINING – Military Press
3-4 x 12-15

AB EXERCISES - Crunches
4 x 25

Wednesday

BICEPS - Standing Barbell Curls
3 x 15

TRICEPS - Lying Overhead Triceps Extensions
4-6 x 15

FOREARM & WRIST – Reverse curls
3 x 15

LEG MUSCLES - Leg Presses
4-8 x 8-15

Lying Leg Curls
3-6 x 8-10

Seated Calf Raises
3-4 x 12

Friday

CHEST – Flat Barbell Bench Presses
1 set x 15 reps
2-3 sets x 10 reps

BACK MUSCLES – Lat Pulldowns
3 sets x 12-15 reps

SHOULDER TRAINING – Side Lateral Raises
3-4 x 12-15

Front Lateral Raises
3-4 x 12-15

Bent Lateral Raises
3-4 x 12-15

AB EXERCISES - Crunches
4 x 25

Routine # 3

6 Day program Chest, Shoulders, Arms, Back, Legs and Abs – change exercises each day

(2 Exercises per body part – there is only one listed here – you need to add the other)

Monday

CHEST - Incline Dumbbell Presses
1 set x 15 reps

2-3 sets x 10 reps

Tuesday

SHOULDER TRAINING – Military Press
3-4 x 12-15

Wednesday

BICEPS - Standing Barbell Curls
3 x 15

TRICEPS - Lying Overhead Triceps Extensions
4-6 x 15

FOREARM & WRIST – Reverse curls
3 x 15

Thursday

BACK MUSCLES - One-Arm Dumbbell Rows
3 sets x 12-15 reps

Friday

LEG MUSCLES - Leg Presses
4-8 x 8-15

Lying Leg Curls
3-6 x 8-10

Seated Calf Raises
3-4 x 12

Saturday

AB EXERCISES - Crunches
4 x 25

The following list is a collection of the books and audio books that have inspired me over the years and in many ways influenced the writing of this book. I invite you to read them all.

Codependent No More/Beyond Codependency – Melanie Beatty

Quantum Healing/Ageless Body, Timeless Mind/Grow Younger, Live Longer/The Seven Spiritual Laws of Success – Deepak Chopra

Bio Markers – William Evans

The Road Less Traveled – M. Scott Peck

Age Proof Your Brain – Tony Buzan

Why God Won't Go Away – Andrew Newberg, Eugene D'Aquili

Emotional Intelligence (Why it can matter more than IQ) – Daniel Goleman

Emotional Intelligence Quick Book – Travis Bradberry, Jean Greaves

7 Habits of Highly Effective People/The 8th Habit – Stephen R. Covey

Body for Life – Bill Phillips, Michael D'Orso

The Power of Now/Stillness Speaks – Eckhart Tolle

Living the Wisdom of the Tao/Change Your Thoughts, Change Your Life/Wayne Dyer CD Collection – Wayne Dyer

The Art of Happiness/Destructive Emotions – HH Dalai Lama & Howard C. Cutler

Top Performance – Zig Ziglar

Awaken the Giant Within – Tony Robbins

How to Win Friends & Influence People – Dale Carnegie

A History of God – Karen Armstrong

Conversations with God – Neale Donald Walsch

The Alchemist/Veronika Decides to Die – Paulo Coelho

The Way of the Peaceful Warrior – Dan Milman

A Course in Miracles – Helen Schucman

The Power of Positive Thinking – Norman Vincent Peale

Think and Grow Rich – Napoleon Hill

Tuesdays with Morrie – Mitch Albom

The Secret of the Ages – Robert Collier

29889332R00129

Made in the USA
San Bernardino, CA
31 January 2016